FACES BEHIND THESE SYSTEMS

Charged with Three Felonies without Committing Any Crime

NK. YAHUSHUA

© Copyright 2019 - All rights reserved.

It is not legal to reproduce, duplicate, or transmit any part of this document in either electronic means or in printed format. Recording of this publication is strictly prohibited and any storage of this document is not allowed unless with written permission from the publisher except for the use of brief quotations in a book review.

CONTENTS

Introduction   v

Chapter One: Before   1
Chapter Two: The Incident   13
Chapter Three: A "Clerical Error"   25
Chapter Four: The Fight   40
Chapter Five: The Fallout   53
Chapter Six: Healing   65
Chapter Seven: Loose Ends   77
Final Words   87

INTRODUCTION

At the time that I am writing this book, the USA is scrambling to manage the effects of a global pandemic while coming off the heels of weeks-long protests against police brutality. Following the recorded murder of George Floyd in Minneapolis, our nation erupted at its seams with protestors on the streets of every major city nationwide demanding immediate action. Meanwhile, on social media, millions of users got a crash course in racial inequality via hundreds of informational posts, shared links, and activists speaking out. In early June, social media platform Instagram was wiped out in solidarity by users who uploaded plain black squares to their accounts. People are consciously deciding to redirect their daily spending toward Black-owned businesses, signing petitions in pursuit of justice, and attempting to educate their families and friends about the realities of systemic racism.

To those of us who have not only been aware of these realities but have lived since birth experiencing them firsthand, it's a curious thing to watch. Why now? Why does the world suddenly want to tell the truth? Perhaps the coast-to-coast stay-at-home orders contributed by sending millions in boredom to the internet, where we all in unison watched the traumatic footage of George Floyd's death by suffocation.

Or maybe it was the unity we all felt at the time as we, for the first time in decades, were forced to slow life down and experience a universal fear of sickness and death. Whatever the cause, the ratio of emotion to attention must have been just right this early summer as everyone seemed to snap out of their stupor all at once. This is not the land of the free until all are equal. I know this well, but it still feels nice to hear everyone else say it aloud.

According to the NAACP, 22% of fatal police shootings are perpetrated against Black people, despite the fact that we make up only 13% of the total U.S. population. There are little known statistics to represent the number of non-fatal shootings and instances of excessive force that are perpetrated against Black people versus non-Black people. Likewise, 34% of the nation's incarcerated population is Black. That's to say nothing about the victims of systemic racism who find themselves once again released into the free world. Reacclimating to life outside prison is a feat so difficult that most are unable to accomplish it. It's no wonder, considering the fact that having any criminal record reduces the likelihood of receiving a job offer by 50%. This so-called democracy, by the people and for the people, seems to be hell-bent on keeping its Black citizens strapped tight between a rock and a hard place. As these statistics continue to get worse year after year, the damaging stereotypes persist, and the cycle perpetuates.

At this point, I don't think there can be any doubt that the American government is objectively and overwhelmingly guilty of using its legislative and penal systems to subjugate a population that has not found respite from prejudice or discrimination since the nation was established in 1776.

I am heartened to feel the shift in our cultural climate as the topic of racism and racial profiling in law enforcement rises to the surface of our country's consciousness. African-American citizens are speaking out in confidence to demand change, while those who aren't privy to our experience take the time to educate themselves on the many iterations of systemic racism that have plagued America for centuries. I watch and listen as protestors discuss cutting police force budgets, implementing prison reform policies, and punishing offending officers to the fullest extent of the law.

Though I am skeptical, I cannot help but allow hope to infiltrate my heart. I hope we'll see real change. I hope these policies will offer protection and safety to the millions of Black American citizens who don't presently have it. Yet all the while, as I watch my nation simmer and boil with righteous indignation, I can't help but notice a huge gap in the public narrative. I am overjoyed that such important and heavy issues are being addressed by the mainstream media, but I am also discouraged by the public's lack of awareness about the people in that gap. I am in that gap.

While America protests against mass incarceration and excessive police force, it fails to recognize that there are survivors of racial profiling who neither die nor serve a long prison sentence. It fails to recognize people like me who are technically living in the "free" world while simultaneously wading through mountains of pitiless red tape just to clear our names. It fails to recognize that, while convicting murderers is surely a worthwhile cause, there are plenty of victims who remain alive and need help just as badly as those who are not. It fails to recognize how effortlessly a law enforcement officer's single callous behavior can leave a person mired in a land void of opportunity, destitute and desperate for relief. It fails to recognize how a tainted criminal record could debilitate a person for the rest of their lives, even if they aren't lying six feet under or sitting behind bars. I'm one of the people waiting here, in the gap, to have my name cleared and my life restored.

Believe it or not, there was a time when I truly believed that American law was fair, that our justice system stayed true to its name, and that opportunity remained available to all who rightfully earned it. It's not true, and I found out the hard way. So, at a time when people finally seem to be listening, I've decided to tell my story.

I came to this decision for several reasons, the first of which is that my story has no ending, at least not yet. I am still in the thick of it. In my case, justice has not been served. Despite my doctoral degree in history and my stacked resume, I cannot find reliable employment in my chosen field. Because of racial profiling, my home went into foreclosure. I lost or was not even granted the opportunity to hold many jobs, and I manage daily the side effects of spending over five years on strong antidepressants. I am telling my story because **I need help.**

I am also telling my story because **I can help**. In circumstances that I would never have chosen myself, I have learned invaluable lessons about how to become a self-advocate amidst a profoundly broken and twisted system. When the world put me in a corner between two stone walls, I somehow found a way to open a door, and then another, and then another. I've never taken the bar exam, but I now know enough about the law to defend myself in front of a state judge. I know what makes a good lawyer, how to identify a person's good or bad intentions, and exactly what my constitutional rights are, down to the letter.

Most importantly, I am telling my story to offer hope, faith, and love to all who want and need it. The psychological effects of this battle I'm fighting against a far more powerful opponent cannot be overstated. I firmly believe that, without my belief in God and my confidence in God's heart for justice, I would not be alive today. When I saw no way out of misery, God lifted me to a bird's eye view. I saw that, while my life on earth has been painful, and at times unbearable, it isn't the only life I have. There's another one after this. So in my own time of need, God called me to serve others. Because of the Lord, I have faith that justice will be served. My name will be cleared.

Dear reader, this one's for all the people in the gap. This one's for the people who can't apply to a job without holding their breath. This one's for the people who are on the professional blacklist. This one's for the people who are waiting to wait so that they can wait in line some more. This one's for the people who have watched their lives implode while they anticipate a too-long postponed day in court. This one's for the people who never had their day in court at all.

This story is for the twenty-something Black kid who would rather take an undeserved penalty than play David against Goliath in a losing fight. This story is for the twenty-something Black kid who should never have been stopped in the first place. This story is for those of us who had the guts to stay the course and are paying the price all over again at the start of each day. We're the invisible middle, living in apartments and homes, waking up to our dogs and a pot of fresh coffee, heading to work at a job for which we're overqualified and underpaid. We're the ones who look free on the outside yet are waiting indefinitely in the purgatory of a stuffy, beige, and endless bureaucratic maze.

We've seen the faces behind the headstones. We've seen the faces behind the bars. But what about us? We're the faces behind these systems. Those sinned against and left for dead.

CHAPTER ONE: BEFORE
Early Life

My story begins long before my birthday. My father was born one of 49 children to an Igbuzo king who kept several wives in the Delta State of Nigeria. My mother, a Nigerian Hebrew-Igbo, was born in the same kingdom. They both, along with the rest of my family, were brought up in the Igbo tradition, which carries with it a mixture of Christian traditions, Jewish practices, and African culture. The Hebrew-Igbo are often referred to as the "lost tribe of Israel," though I never had any trouble locating any of my relatives at all, as we all remained extremely close, even on different continents.

My own ancestors lived lives of privilege, joy, and abundance in a nation that originated, uplifted, and celebrated our identities. After meeting and marrying, my parents immigrated to the United States to put down roots in Chicago, Illinois. I would soon be born in Hyde Park, the second of seven children and one of six daughters. I was named after my father's mother, Buashie, and blessed with a large familial network of support.

I would spend the early years of my childhood in Chicago with my small but growing family, attending preschool at St. Thomas the Apostle Catholic School and cultivating the love of learning that would carry me through life. When I was four years old, my parents decided to temporarily relocate my sister and me to Ibusa so that we could all convene in my father's childhood home with his aging parents.

This highly concentrated time spent with my relatives revealed much about my own father's origins. As members of the ruling class in an oil-producing state, my father's family led a lifestyle bursting with travel, business, culture, and art. My father, much like myself, was frequently and from a young age exposed to creativity, intellect, and politics. His mother, after whom I was named, was the glue that kept our large family returning to one another and maintaining strong relationships.

My namesake had a life that few here in America could possibly imagine as one of many co-wives to an Igbo king. She lived her life according to the Bible and frequently set aside her own negative feelings to cultivate a safe environment for her children. As I learned about healthy and unhealthy attachment styles later in my adult life, I would hearken back to these days spent in my grandmother's home and marvel at her intuitive parenting decisions, the way she gathered all members of the family around the dining table for each meal, how often she chose forgiveness over separation, and her general attitude of acceptance and love. Spending some of my most formative years beneath my grandmother's roof helped my little girl's heart to feel grounded, safe, and loved. My healthy roots, tended to so early by my Grandmother OnyekamBuashie, are one of many things that have kept me alive and determined through the many trials I have faced.

While many Hebrew-Igbo mothers nurtured me at home, Catholic sisters guided me in school. I attended Maryland Comprehensive Catholic School in Lagos and had much of the groundwork for my strong Christian faith laid by priests and nuns. Contrary to the many stereotypes about Catholic schooling, life at Maryland Comprehensive did not feel religiously restrictive. The faith was presented to me, but not projected onto me. I watched, listened, and absorbed. My father, who had taken a position as the Assistant Dean of Mass Communication at the University of Lagos, infused my childhood moments with intellectual challenges, creative outlets, and more than enough space for imagination.

Ironically, I didn't find God in Catholic school. I found God on the afternoons and weekends when I joined my dance team for a practice or recital. I found God inside my own body as it moved to the music, propelled by the energy of my breathing, and miraculously formed beautiful shapes and rhythms as a result. I excelled as a dancer and discovered the arts of leadership and cooperation through my relationships with my peers. Following in my grandmother's footsteps, I learned to approach the small conflicts of a child's life with a staunch allegiance to forgiveness, resolution, and love. I learned that I could trust myself, my mind, my breath, and my body to deliver through dance the things I had so often kept locked in the confines of my mind. There in my grandparents' village, I came to understand the power of mental presence, concentration, and faith.

During these formative years in Nigeria, my mother and father experienced many conflicts in their marriage. They traveled between the U.S. and Nigeria several times, so my sister and I spent lots of time living with our grandmother as our primary caregiver. My parents ultimately separated, and as I emerged into my preteen years, my father remarried with hopes of providing his two daughters with a reliable mother figure. Soon my older sister and I returned to Hyde Park in Chicago so that I could attend high school at Kenwood Academy in South Chicago while my older sister began pursuing her college degree.

Of my early childhood, I'll say this: I believe that children are born with open minds that, in many circumstances, are encouraged to close by strict parental expectations, a lack of cultural exposure, or some mixture of the two. The way I grew up, imbued with several diverse ideologies, cultures, and environments, maintained the natural openness of my innocent mind. I am eternally grateful for this. In my life, I have seen that the common denominator of intolerance, violence, and disunion is close-mindedness. Thanks to God and the life the Lord gave me, I can find love, humanity, and tolerance in any person, no matter their religious, cultural, ethnic, or social background.

Leaving Home

As a teenager in the city, life felt a bit lackluster compared to my experiences in the village. The mother figure that my father had hoped to introduce into our lives was anything but. She often physically and emotionally abused me without my father's knowledge. Adapting to a world that felt so unsafe from a childhood that had been soaked through with loving connection and supportive attachment proved difficult for me. I was expected to navigate puberty and adolescence with grace and to excel in school, all while enduring the verbal and physical attacks of a person I should have been able to trust.

After my parents' separation, I had wanted to rediscover a sense of normalcy in my own life and the lives of my parents. So when the abuse started, I was reluctant to disclose it to my father. I wanted him to have a partner, and I certainly didn't want to be the reason for introducing conflict into our home. Nevertheless, my father found out how his new wife was treating me and chose to remove her from our lives. While this was a tumultuous decision for my father, my siblings, and me, it was also a great act of love that solidified my trust in my father. He resolved himself to life as a single parent and would not marry again until all of his children were safely delivered into adulthood.

Relying on the strength of the love I had felt as a young girl, I did not allow the pain of this negative relationship to break me. I excelled in high school and set my sights on attending the University of California at Los Angeles after graduating at 17. I longed for the warmth and sun of California and knew that this prestigious college would thrust me happily into a secure professional future. Though I had indicated in my application that I would need campus accommodations such as dormitory housing and a meal plan, I was informed upon my acceptance that there was no space for me to enjoy either. My mother stood against sending me so far away to live in an apartment without the security of the university system's policies, which gravely disappointed me but nevertheless influenced my decision to forgo moving to L.A. and attend community college in Illinois.

Though I longed to exchange the seasons of the American midwest for the year-round sunlight of California, I made the most of my early college years by joining my childhood best friends Lenice, Adele, Vashti and her sister, Darling, for many nights and weekends of nonstop adolescent fun. We socialized, laughed, and enjoyed our newfound independence while, as always, meeting our parents' high expectations for academic performance. When I wanted to move past the ways of my upbringing, I would turn to my longtime friend Vashti, whom I had met as a sophomore at Kenwood. Vashti and I often delighted in our mutual agreement to press past social expectations and to discuss those topics which had been labeled taboo by our parents back home. We spent time delving into the more complicated topics of religion, politics, and relationships. Like so many young adults, I began to move past what I had been taught throughout my childhood and grow into my truest self.

All the while, I attended classes and remained attentive to the things I was hearing and learning in each session. Soon I learned that the Chicago public school system, specifically its public college network, was experiencing financial shortages and cutting budgets across the city. I wanted to do more than theorize and wonder—I wanted to do something. Again I came back to my belief that education and diversification are the antidotes to intolerance and close-mindedness, and I knew that cutting funding for education there in my home city would do nothing to bring union to our communities. I set off on a seven-month tour of grassroots organizations, raising awareness about the upcoming budget cuts and organizing groups of students to attend city hall forums and political rallies. In the meantime, I founded an on-campus organization called Voices of Tomorrow to help provide resources to students who were in need of supplies and aid due to a lack of academic funding. Through this organization during my years at community college, we hosted politicians such as Senator Braun and Barack Obama. Though there were many opportunities offered to me within the world of Chicago politics, I knew I wouldn't be spending my adult life in the area and turned many down, keeping my sights set on California. I went on to attend Southern Illinois University at Carbondale, where I maintained my momentum by seeking more professional growth. I strengthened my skills as an activist and continued to explore my spiritual leanings toward Christianity.

I graduated with a Bachelor of Science in Political Science from Southern Illinois University and moved to Philadelphia to begin graduate school.

My Twenties on the East Coast

I spent some of my early twenties there in Philadelphia trying my hand at spoken word poetry and establishing myself in the city's art and music scene. I met many local artists who would go on to accomplish great things in the years to come, from Jill Scott to Musiq Soulchild, The Roots, BlackStar, Erykah Badu to Common, and Zap Mama. I dated, socialized, and enjoyed my independence.

At around the same time that a romantic relationship of mine was turning sour, my little brother, Jioha called me up to inform me that he had just accepted his dream job at Goldman Sachs in New York City. As my connections in Philadelphia tapered off, I felt like there would be no better time than the present to try my hand as a New Yorker. I was already commuting to the city on a weekly basis to see live music shows, and living with my brother would allow us both to save on rent. With no reason to stay and nothing to lose, I packed my bags and headed north.

Once I had settled in Brooklyn, I began teaching as a substitute at several local elementary schools while seeking my next step toward career development. I accepted a position as the marketing manager for The Truth, an anti-tobacco organization headquartered there in the city. I spent my personal time enjoying New York's live music scene with my friends Anita and Steve, as well as my brilliantly talented friends QueenGodis, Sister Noni and Mecca Starr, returning to the childhood bliss of breath and movement through regular yoga and pilates classes, and burning off steam at a boxing gym to stay in shape. Again I sought and found social connections, dated off and on, and generally basked in the carefree life of a young educated woman in the metropolis.

It was in my early twenties in Philadelphia that I met Nna for the first time. My boyfriend brought him home to me, a little sick puppy with a swollen belly and bald, scaly skin patches from a bad case of mange. "He needs your healing touch," my boyfriend had said hopefully while placing Nna into my arms. Immediately, I was in love. I knew I had found a reliable companion to keep me grounded. Eventually, I'd let that boyfriend go, but I always kept Nna right by my side.

Nna was a mutt who had all the prominent physical features of a pit bull terrier. As he grew into an adult, his little starving belly leveled out, his mange-eaten skin healed to grow fur, and he grew fully into his doggy form. He was stocky with a square muzzle, wide head, and athletic build. His temperament couldn't have been better, as I was able to socialize and train him from a very young age. Sadly, however, when I'd take him for potty breaks or walks around the streets of Brooklyn, passersby would cross the street to avoid passing by the two of us. They perceived him as a threat with his strong jaw and prideful gait, though that couldn't have been further from the truth. Nna was truly an ambassador for the pit bull terrier breed. He was loyal, gentle, intelligent, and eager to please.

In a place that is reputed to be the center of progressive politics and universal acceptance, my fellow citizens never thought twice about stereotyping poor Nna into the worst possible representation of his breed. It saddened me and made me think critically about human psychology. I wondered how many good experiences people, including myself, may have missed due to their failure to ask questions, suspend assumptions, and acknowledge the intrinsic individuality of the humans (and animals) that we encounter on an everyday basis. So many times, I watched pedestrians avoid Nna when they could have just as easily bent down to receive one of his sloppy, happy greetings.

For the umpteenth time, I resolved myself to remain open-minded and accepting in this life so as to not miss the opportunities that so many less accepting people were missing all around me. Sometimes I look back to those many Brooklyn walks and wonder how things might be different if only I could have predicted how relevant this lesson would become in the following years.

A Near Miss

In the late summer of 2001, I decided to take a trip back to Chicago to visit my family. As usual, I traveled to Philadelphia with Nna so that my friend Noni could look after him for the duration of my trip. A few moments of doggy bowls, leash transfers, and giving details about Nna's routine were all we had before I gave his head a loving scratch and then boarded a red-eye flight to Chicago.

After touchdown, drowsy, and longing for a bed, I got off the plane and ambled through the airport, down the escalator, and out the doors into the fresh morning air of my hometown. I caught a cab to my mother's home and took a sigh of relief as I parked my suitcase and fell happily into a spreading sleep, unencumbered by the narrow seats and restrictive armrests that I'd battled against the night before. The date was September 11th.

My sleep was harshly interrupted when my mother burst through the bedroom door with the landline phone held to her ear as my younger sister Yem's muffled screams carried through the receiver. She was calling from her home on the campus at Howard University, begging frantically to know where I was.

"Where is NK?! Where is NK?!" she shouted as she watched the Twin Towers billow with smoke on her television screen. Though she had heard me come in hours before, my mother—disoriented by her daughter's hysteria— still needed to confirm what she already knew. I was safe in her home, fast asleep, but waking unsoundly to the graceless commotion. Following my younger sister's orders, my mother turned on the television in the living room. We stood together in silence as the second plane smashed into the towers over live broadcast. For a brief moment, I caught a glimpse of the gray silhouette of a Boeing 767 aircraft. It was the same one I had disembarked from so early that morning. In horror and confusion, I watched as the plane and building converged into one calamitous collapse.

Though I was hundreds of miles away from the disaster, I still felt curiously close to death there in my mother and step-father's cozy living room. I remembered the mundane whistle of that plane's air conditioning, the muted ding of its seatbelt lights, the smell of carpet and coffee. I remembered the faces of the flight attendants who had offered me juice and ginger ale. I remembered the signs of life on that plane, the periodic whooshing of the toilet in the back, the low whispers of groggy passengers. We had been strangers in close proximity for only a few hours, now forever tied by one somber knowing; we had brushed against the Grim Reaper on that gray, cold vessel. I wondered if anyone had remained on that plane for its final voyage back to New York City. I grieved for those lost and wilted in a strange soup of shame for having survived. I prayed.

A week later, as my visit concluded and I once again made that pilgrimage between Chicago and New York City by plane, everything felt different. The air in the airport practically pulsed with distress as many travelers wordlessly moved about, nervously awaiting their own ascension into airspace. The narrow seats and restrictive armrests now felt less like nuisances and more like a dark, unknown risk. As we neared the city and lowered past the cloud covering, I saw the gaping hole where two towers had once stood tall and shuddered at the still-rising gray smoke. "This would have been my grave," I whispered to myself. I held a moment of silence there in my heart for the many souls, full of hopes and hurts and loved ones' names, that had watched helplessly as their lives took one sharp and final turn toward a pair of cherished monuments. I would never be the same.

Moving West

Once I was home again with Nna, I tried to find my old sense of normalcy in a city that, quite literally, had the ground shifting beneath it. I marveled at the unity of the human spirit as the entire city rose to serve by praying, memorializing, and rebuilding our collective home. I acclimated, like everyone around me, to the new melancholy that lingered out on the streets and in the parks. Even the Statue of Liberty seemed to have lowered her eyes in mourning.

Meanwhile, in my personal life, I struggled to come to terms with what I viewed as a message from the Divine. I felt as though God had reached a hand out toward me and whispered in the still small voice of my heart, "This is your second chance." I remembered the dreams of my youth, my aspirations to live near the sun and ocean waves in California, my abiding fondness for intellect and academia, and the ever-shortening expanse of my life. After much consideration through fasting, prayer, and solitude, I reached my conclusion: I would move out west to Los Angeles, where I had really always been heading. I could feel the 18-year-old me smile and bubble over with excitement during the winter of 2002 as I made plans to travel cross-country, Nna in tow, to take up new residence in the Sunshine State.

Back in 1999, I had gone to visit a colleague who worked in the L.A. branch of The Truth. He lived in the Los Feliz neighborhood, which enchanted me through the lens of my windshield when I visited for the first time. I loved how sprawling and earthy the area felt despite being mere miles from the urbane trappings of the city in the valley. The noise that accosted my senses on Hollywood Boulevard dulled to a peaceful hum once we crossed over into Los Feliz, and I bookmarked its community feel in my brain files for later use.

Since I was not local to the area, I was not at all familiar with Los Feliz's reputation for housing wealthier citizens and having a higher standard of living. I only remember the facial expression and body language of an acquaintance, a caucasian male, whom I was sharing dinner with during my visit when I told him how I planned to spend my time in the city. I explained that I'd be visiting a friend's mother's salon on Slauson Avenue, and watched his face contort into a vague expression of distaste as he asked in disbelief, "You're going *down there?*"

Later, when I disclosed my plans to meet the colleague in Los Feliz in conversation with my friend's mother, who is African-American, while visiting her salon on Slauson, her eyebrows raised in a gesture of haughty surprise as she lilted the end of her question "Wow, you're going *up there?*"

I sensed something off-kilter in the shifting postures of her facial features and body, but couldn't quite pin their meaning down to any particular implication. Still, the memory of those two questions with their embedded directional references stuck with me. Clearly, to the locals, Slauson was low while Los Feliz was high. I took note.

Later that winter, I returned to my heart's home again. While

CHAPTER ONE: BEFORE

exploring L.A. in my rental car, I got lost and wound up somewhere in Griffith Park. I imagined Nna's wide panting mouth running through the hills, surrounded by Hollywood history and the breathtaking landscape. I knew that I wanted this geography to be a regular fixture in my life. I knew I would move there someday.

When someday came, I knew just where to go. I lived on Edgemont Street and could see both Griffith Observatory and Brad Pitt's home if I tilted my chin to the hilltops. I hiked twice a week and made lots of time to browse the art gallery shows in the area. For four years, I basked in the bliss of having trucked a dream into fruition. I stayed up to date with community events and attended as many as I could. I was a regular at the local flea market as I decorated and nested in my new apartment. About once a month, my neighbor and friend Sherry Jennings and I'd pack our favorite bottle of wine, a collection of cheeses and crackers, and a picnic blanket to attend live theater events in the park. I was free from obligation, excelling at my job, and swirling in gratitude for all the things I'd worked so hard to attain. I lived close enough to the ocean, under the sun, and covered in grace.

Speaking of grace, I held tight to my faith even after moving to this new, radical place. While my ambition and leisure found solace in Los Feliz and the trails of Griffith Park, my spirituality found its anchor at Agape International Spiritual Center in Culver City. I immediately became involved as a church usher. I believe that the best way to stay accountable and responsible as a follower of God is to take on commitments within the church family. Each Sunday and sometimes more often, I arrived to serve the house of the Lord with a smile on my face and no reason to let it fade. I developed many supportive friendships there, namely with Reverend Michael Beckwith and his wife Rickky. I earned the nickname FancyFace there at church and delighted in seeing all the faces of my newfound family as they filed into the building each week.

When 2007 arrived, I was standing firm on strong foundations. I was physically healthy, plugged into my community, loved by a healthy and well-trained Nna, and focused on my lifelong spiritual journey. That May, my beloved Griffith Park caught fire and burned for two days. When it was safe, I returned to my old hiking trails and prayed for God's favor to restore the land. Ironically, I'd watched my own life begin to burn in that same park just a couple of years prior.

CHAPTER SUMMARY

- I am born, growing in love between Hyde Park, Ibusa, and Lagos, Nigeria.
- My parents divorce in the 80s
- I earn my Bachelors degree from Southern Illinois University in Carbondale
- I adopt Nna in New York City and nurse him back to health
- I get off the Boeing 767 on September 11th that will go on to crash into the Twin Towers, gaining a new lease on life
- I move to L.A. in December 2002

In the next chapter, you will learn how I was racially profiled, falsely imprisoned, and unjustly penalized in an incident that would forever alter my life for the worse.

CHAPTER TWO: THE INCIDENT

My move to L.A. did have a little more to it than just a girl following her dreams. In those last months back in New York, I had met a guy. He was flashy, gorgeous, and social, plus we had lots of things in common. He, too, had spent some years of his childhood growing up in Nigeria, knew the places and the land, and the people that I looked on with such fondness when remembering my childhood years. Coincidentally, we had both been flown back to America from Nigeria in the same year. This man—let's call him Leo—was also a well-known actor in a famous sitcom at the time. He was just the sort of person I wanted to meet. He reminded me of home without losing his charm or mystery. I was enchanted. The only hitch? Leo lived in L.A., and I still lived in Brooklyn.

The night we met, Leo had asked me to accompany him to a nice restaurant in the city as his date. We enjoyed delicious food in a group setting, and from that day forward, whenever we could, we visited one another and talked. As our relationship escalated in intensity, Leo asked me to move to the West Coast to be with him. It had always been my goal to move to the valley, but something about doing it this way didn't sit right with me. I told Leo that I liked him and wanted to continue dating, but I wouldn't move to California on these terms. I needed to make that move on my own time. I needed to choose my own apartment and neighborhood, find my own friends, and create my own home. I didn't want to live my dream in someone else's home with someone else's friends, someone else's life. I wanted to build my own.

Upon receiving this news, Leo immediately closed off from me. I could feel it. He had taken my answer as an outright rejection of his intimate offer, though I never intended it that way. Our romance began to stale, but we continued connecting and visiting one another. One day, a few months following our conversation, I was set to fly out to Southern California to see Leo. We had arranged the dates and planned to spend time together. Yet when I got off the plane, he was not there to greet me and take me to his apartment. I found my way out of the maze and took a car to his building, where I found out that he was involved with someone else. The "someone" was currently in his apartment. It became clear to me that Leo's pride mattered more to him than any connection we may have had together.

As mentioned before, I did eventually move to Los Angeles, but Leo and I had drifted so far apart at that point that I felt no need to break the news. That is until I discovered through mutual friends that he was not only aware of my relocation but was living in the same neighborhood as me. In L.A., it's every local's habit to peer into vehicles as they pass by, considering there are hundreds of A-list celebrities milling about and living their normal lives. On my weekly hikes, I often saw Leo out and about in Los Feliz. Regardless, I only viewed him now as someone I used to know.

One Sunday, I saw Leo at the Agape Spiritual Center and said hello. We began to warm back up to one another, but put no labels on our relationship as we wanted to remove the pressure from our interactions. Still, we often sat together once I had finished my ushering duties on Sunday mornings. At the same time, I had run into an old college girlfriend in L.A. and began spending more time with her. I invited her to church with me, where she briefly met Leo in the sanctuary. Even though this friend had a reputation for dishonoring girl code back in school, I thought nothing of their short introduction and forgot it had happened as soon as it was over. After a few months of enjoying these two rekindled relationships, my intuition began to sound off that something was amiss. So one Sunday, guided by the gentle tugging of my instinct, I broke my usual ushering routine and walked outside the sanctuary. There, I saw Leo and my friend together. Their body language indicated that they were very comfortable with one another. Too comfortable. I confronted them and lost both my love interest and my close friend in one gloomy swoop. They had apparently been sexually involved for weeks and had been routinely attending the earlier church service together before Leo inconspicuously took his seat next to me at the late morning service after. When I got up to usher our attendees out of the sanctuary, Leo had been sneaking out the opposite door to meet with my friend. I had caught them in the act. Once the initial anger passed, I was left with a sense of betrayal and a feeling of deep, lonely sorrow. I began spending my weekends alone with Nna once again.

That's the NK. who was hiking in Griffith Park in the early autumn of 2004. With my social circle recently fractured, I felt guarded and skeptical toward the world, so I went where I always went when I needed some happy sweat and time inside Mother Nature's embrace. The park's sandy terrain rose around me like a gentle hug as its green and gray brambles entangled with one another, climbing up the textured hills. The setting sun shone down on my skin and started beads of sweat pricking on my nose, hairline, and shoulders. My feet crunched in auditory bliss against the land beneath me as I savored the familiar thrill of this California earth, the particular piece of earth I had longed to encounter since the age of 17. They say that when something happens to change your life, whether it's a wedding or a funeral, the birth of a child or a personal tragedy, you immediately begin dividing your life's experience into **before** and **after.** I didn't know it, but these were my last few treasured moments in the before.

Guilty Until Proven Innocent

Since Nna and I were regulars in the park, he knew the route and was well-behaved off-leash. As I mentioned before, we'd hike together multiple times a week. He stayed within a small radius of me and enjoyed all the new smells as I walked behind him. There were no signs in the park that communicated any city ordinance or leash law. Nna had a reliable recall and was so friendly with dogs and people alike that I didn't feel any reluctance unclipping his lead once we'd made it safely onto the trail. After all, Griffith Park isn't your usual grassy urban green space. It's hilly, sandy, rocky, and huge. Wildlife roams free through the trails, from mountain lions to snakes to any number of rodents and birds. Nna was the least of any visitor's worries.

Unfortunately, no matter how confident or familiar I felt in this place, the tables could turn in a second. And that afternoon, they did. A park ranger rapidly approached me, my friend Rae, and her son Nubia, and began pressing us with indirect questions. After answering a few, I asked in confusion, "What exactly do you need? Is there a problem?" In response, the officer became very direct with his inquiries, most of which were now directed toward Nna's free roaming. "Why isn't the dog on the leash?" he demanded.

I began explaining our familiarity with the area, Nna's good nature, and the fact that countless other visitors accompanied by untethered dogs. The ranger became increasingly agitated, repeating his questions and frustratedly stating that I should have my dog on a leash. As the situation intensified, I only got more confused. I couldn't understand why this ranger found our presence in the park so upsetting. We were two grown women, one Black, one white, and one young boy of mixed race.

I knew enough about America's social climate to expect that Black and African-American *men* would face discrimination due to their race and gender. I knew that this country consistently assumed that men with darker complexions were dangerous. I was living in post 9/11 America, where the term Muslim seemed to be inextricably linked with criminality and violence. I had seen racism in action, and I knew that my male relatives and love interests with darker skin faced a suffocating stigma when out in public. I knew that no matter their personalities, histories, families, or intentions, people would often treat them as criminals. Still, I had not anticipated that it would happen to me.

Other visitors curiously looked on as they passed our awkwardly arranged group, some with their free roaming dogs, others alone and enjoying the nice weather like we had intended to do upon arriving. Though it was clear there was some sort of verbal altercation occurring, no one stepped in to ask questions or offer support. We were surrounded by people and completely alone.

I caught myself nervously laughing at the situation as I answered the officer's questions. The entire situation seemed so ludicrous. Soon after the ranger had approached, I had recalled Nna and clipped his leash onto his harness. Not only did this prove my compliance with the officer's wishes, but it also demonstrated Nna's listening skills and his reliable training. Griffith Park might as well have been my home for the number of hours I'd spent climbing its heights, smelling its greenery, and even praying over its ashes when it had burned earlier that year. When it became clear that the officer was no longer willing to be rational in his approach to us, I decided it might just be better to cut our evening short and head back home. "Okay," I turned and said to my friend and her son, "Let's just go home." We turned to begin backtracking toward my apartment.

"No." The officer said firmly. "Let me see your ID."

I couldn't believe it. My mind raced as I tried to understand. It was clear to me at this point that the officer's behavior was not motivated by any genuine concern for safety—at least, not for our safety. He was buckling down on a situation that I had been trying to resolve quickly, quietly, and with as much civility as possible. I couldn't turn around and go back to my home without disobeying the commands of a law enforcement officer. This sudden loss of such a simple freedom terrified me, but I knew the only way out of this officer's deadlocked grip was through. I searched for my ID and realized that I didn't have it. I lived so close to Griffith Park that I usually just walked to the trailheads from my apartment, and since my friend had met me there, I hadn't needed my license for anything. I had left it at home.

See, that's not how things are supposed to work in this country. Our identification cards, whether driver's license, passport, or birth certificate, are meant to serve a purpose. I only need my license when I'm driving. I only need my passport when I'm flying. I am not required by any law to carry an identification document with me to my neighborhood park. I have nothing to prove.

But that's not how I felt as I stood under the gaze of this white male officer. I felt very much like I needed to explain myself, make excuses for my very understandable and unproblematic decision to spend time outdoors. Deep down, my intuition shouted at me, "This isn't right, something isn't right," but the me on the surface was beginning to sweat and just wanted to do anything necessary to escape the rising tension of this confrontation. My heart rate increased as I told the officer that I didn't have my ID on my person. I couldn't meet his requests even if I wanted to. We had arrived at a dead-end, but somehow I knew this wasn't over.

The officer resumed his line of vague and senseless questioning. He wouldn't release us. We were all three too afraid to try walking away from him. Though none of us were handcuffed yet, the ranger held us steadily and forcefully with his domineering presence. He continued to harass us. Thanks to my many years of education in political science and history, I knew my rights. I knew I was free to go unless this officer had grounds to detain me. And he didn't.

"Are you detaining us, sir?" I asked through the thick of his meandering queries. Curdling with anxiety on the inside and standing tall on the outside, I uttered an addendum: "If you aren't detaining me, I'm going home," I said as I again tugged gently on Nna's leash and began to turn around.

The officer closed the space between us and physically restrained me with his forearm, placing it in front of my torso. "You're not going anywhere," he barked.

At that point, my fight or flight response was triggered. I felt cornered, and suddenly all my education, my social status, and my blooming career meant nothing. My constitutional rights meant nothing. I was at the mercy of a park ranger who was not only physically stronger than me but also associated with an organization that could treat me as it wished without consequence. The psychological effects of my perceived helplessness began to sink in as I continued to try to explain myself. "My name is NK," I pleaded.

"I live really close to here. I walked here. I am only taking a hike. My name is NK."

None of it mattered. The officer said he didn't believe that I was

CHAPTER TWO: THE INCIDENT

telling the truth. He stepped away to call his partner into the location, as though I were some sort of violent criminal. I couldn't understand how a relaxing Friday afternoon in my own local park could so abruptly shift into the caged feeling I was experiencing now. Under state law, I could have walked away at any moment. I had committed no crime and was not informed of any grounds for my arrest. But the officer had treated me with such hostility that I felt frozen there in time, even as he turned his back to speak with his colleague. I had never felt more stuck.

Once the second officer arrived, they took my keyring from me. I relied on those keys for access to my car, my home, and my office. Knowing now that I was scared into submission, the men left me standing in the parking lot while they took my keys to each dormant vehicle, testing to see if any belonged to me. They were trying to prove that I had driven to the park without a license. There was absolutely no linear progression to their inexplicable interest in me. I had been stopped by the first park ranger due to Nna's free roaming. Somehow, less than an hour later, I had my personal property unlawfully removed from my possession so that these rangers could prove their unfounded suspicion that I had driven without a driver's license. The mixture of disbelief, outrage, and nervous fear that swirled in my chest was almost too much to bear as I anxiously waited to see their next move.

Before long, the sun began to sink behind the hills as evening rushed in. "You've got to be kidding me," I whispered under my breath. I didn't think it was possible, but anxiety began to rise once again with the passing of time. Not only was I stranded in a dark place with two law enforcement officers, but I was also stranded with two large men. I became acutely aware of their ability to physically overpower me and shifted on my feet, antsy to go somewhere well-lit and full of people. I needed to get somewhere safe. My coworker, who had joined me for this supposed-to-be hike, was equally shocked and immobile by our current circumstances. She had nothing to offer me, as she was managing her own rising adrenaline and anxiety. We waited, powerless.

Unable to match my keys with any of the cars on the premises, the two officers came back toward us to start again from square one. Again

I told them I had walked from my nearby apartment, that I didn't have an ID, and disclosed my full name. At this point, it was clear that this stubborn pair weren't interested in finding a solution, so I searched for one myself. "Call the police," I suggested, "tell them to run my name. I promise you; this is my name. I don't know what else to do."

The officers appeared to take my advice, but no police ever came. It was getting cold. I got brave. "I feel unsafe here. You have two options. Either I am leaving to return to my home, or you're taking me to a police station. You cannot keep me here." I was loaded into their government vehicle alone while my friend, her son, and a very confused Nna took my keys to handle things at home. In hindsight, I'm not quite sure how it was decided upon that I was the sole perpetrator of whatever mystery crime was in question. It seemed a tacit understanding between the officers that I, the African-American woman of the bunch, was the one they would apprehend. As I sat silently in their vehicle, I became restless. I had expected to be taken to the LAPD headquarters mere miles away. Ten minutes turned to 30 as the vehicle's tires continued to hum down the pavement. I had no idea where they were taking me.

After what felt like a lifetime there in the backseat, we arrived at the Van Nuys police department five cities away. Once again, I was dumbfounded. For two individuals employed by a supposedly organized government system, these officers seemed to have no rhyme or reason to their actions at all. Why did I need to be taken to a police station outside my own local jurisdiction? I had neither been arrested nor given grounds for detainment, yet I was presently very much detained there in that foreign, fluorescent building miles from home. Without asking any questions, the on-duty officers booked me into the small jail. I was fingerprinted, photographed, and locked behind bars. All for an off-leash dog?

Because it was a Friday night, I could not see a judge until the following Monday. Whether this was coincidence or collaboration, I couldn't say. If I hadn't had a strong support system or the money to post bail, I would have spent the weekend in that small dingy cell without any information about my own supposed crimes. Thankfully,

I had both money and friends and was able to grant myself freedom. I was set to arrive in Hollywood court first thing Monday.

Before I explain what happened there, I want to pause and address something that I feel is too often overlooked. While I was able to sleep in my own home that weekend, reunite with my dear Nna and gather myself in a safe space, the emotional trauma of the event did not magically slough off my shoulders when I walked out the doors of the small police station. Racial profiling has financial, technical, and occupational side effects, certainly. But more importantly, events like this one send a toxic message to the person who endures them.

To be living a life of abundance in one glorious moment and find yourself completely disenfranchised the next, is no small matter. It has the power to break a human spirit. I come from a loving family with a stable income, abundant knowledge, blessed children, and strong roots. At the time of my false imprisonment, I held a Master's degree and was pursuing a Doctorate. By the laws of American culture, I should have been safe from such a gross miscarriage of justice. Yet, by the flawed judgment of a prejudiced government employee, I lost all social capital in a second. To him, I wasn't an educated, supported, well-cherished community member and child of God. I wasn't the smiling face of an usher at church. I wasn't the helpful coworker, the loving daughter, or the ambitious student. In the eyes of prejudice, I wasn't human at all.

Even if nothing else had come from my experience in the park, it would have taken time to mentally and emotionally recover from the immediate loss of freedom I experienced that night. If I could prevent any person from feeling the way I felt that day as my favorite hiking trail suddenly became the setting of my worst nightmare, I would. No one could help me at that moment. Not the constitution, not the police, not my protective father or my supportive friend. I was completely alone and at the mercy of a person who did not seem to care for my humanity, much less my safety. This is what our country needs to understand. Those who lose their lives to systematic racism are irrevocably wounded, but it is no less painful for those of us who face racial profiling and survive. The psychological repercussions are grave.

The madness continued there in court when I arrived to discover that the name on my case file was Jane Doe. I had been fingerprinted, photographed, and run through the computer system on the night I was booked into Van Nuys's county jail. Everyone should have known at that point that I was who I said I was. But, since part of the officers' complaint against me was that I wouldn't provide an accurate name or identification, this information was ignored, and my name was indicated as unknown. I couldn't help but crack a sardonic smile when I heard this.

When the judge asked whether I wanted a public defender, I immediately refused and informed him that I'd be representing myself. In my mind, the senseless nature of this situation was so obvious that I saw no need to take up a lawyer's time. It should have been clear that there were no grounds for my arrest. I should have been offered an apology. Naively I had hoped that the two officers were the only ones lost in the delusion that I deserved to be imprisoned for letting my dog off his leash. To my dismay, I discovered that the judge wasn't any better as he threatened to deport me should I refuse a public defender. I felt like I was watching my life play out on some ludicrous reality show. How could I be deported? I was born and raised in Chicago. I had full American citizenship. First, I had been accused of lying about my name. Now, I was being profiled as an immigrant due to the African origins of my name. Nothing was making any sense.

I kept hoping, as I scanned the faces in the courtroom, that someone would see the insanity of what was happening. Unfortunately, even as I complied with the judge's demands and selected a public defender, I was only met with more accusations and negative interactions.

During our first meeting, my lawyer started right in with loaded questions that implied my guilt in the situation. "Why didn't you have your dog on the leash?" she asked. "Why didn't you just give them your name?" Whatever hope was left simply escaped from my chest as I began to lose heart. The truth became more and more obscured with each interaction. I urged my lawyer to access the audiotape of my interaction with the park ranger since it was clear that no one respected my voice enough to believe me. What should have been a fervent apology meeting that Monday morning turned into more threats, more recrimination, and more violation.

As the court appointments piled up, I struggled to balance my work on writing a dissertation with pursuing acquittal from a crimeless conviction. My performance at Temple University naturally suffered due to my personal distress with this bizarre legal battle. Soon, my unsupportive public defender made a deal with the city that I would "get off" with paying court fees, serving 60 hours of community service, and agreeing to two years of probation.

What was in it for me, you might ask? I would have my criminal record expunged. I began to suspect that everyone on my case, including my own lawyer, was singularly interested in clearing the two impudent officers' names. I knew that what had happened to me had no justification according to the law. I knew that any reason those officers may have given for arresting me had now been revealed as false. I also knew how detrimental it would be for the city's department of justice if they acknowledged this blatant occurrence of racial profiling and false imprisonment. Still, I was only a kid, and I knew I was significantly outnumbered.

Exhausted by how the very same system that is supposed to be just while they are working against the same justice they want me and the rest of American citizens and foreigners to follow. I accepted that I had my dog off leash in a park but pleaded not GUILTY! I will do their community services and accept to report back after 24 months of penalties as a quick escape from the prolonged bureaucratic nonsense of my situation. Hingsight, I was young and improperly advised. This was my first encounter with the mania of America's self-serving legislative branch, and I didn't know how to advocate for myself. As sad as it sounds today, I saw these exorbitant penalties as the light at the end of the tunnel. I just wanted it to all be over.

The joke was on me. It still isn't over.

CHAPTER SUMMARY

- I am betrayed by a friend, a love interest, which leaves me feeling distrustful of the world.
- I am stopped by a park ranger for having my dog, Nna, off-leash in Griffith Park.
- I am falsely imprisoned in a jail five counties away from my home jurisdiction.
- I am penalized in Hollywood Court and put on a two-year probation, plus paying court fees and serving 60 hours of community service.

In the next chapter, you will learn how this single blatant injustice snowballed due to a clerical error, landing me effectively on the Hollywood blacklist as unhireable.

CHAPTER THREE: A "CLERICAL ERROR"

As with any life-altering event, it would take me a while to process what had happened to me that night at Griffith Park. I served my hours of community service, paid my fees, and showed up early to each meeting. My life, which had previously been peppered with frequent travels and carefree engagement with the outside world, was now barred by curfews and required disclosures. I felt like a bug caught under someone's thumb, wriggling, and striving to reach freedom to no avail. I couldn't forgive and forget and return to the life I had before, because my freedom had become conditional.

No matter how many times I reassured myself that I hadn't broken any laws that day, I struggled with shame beneath my new label as a criminal. I had been charged with resisting arrest, falsely representing myself, and permitting a pet off-leash. After listening to the audiotape of my confrontation with the park ranger, during which I both complied with requests and offered my legal name, the judge dropped all charges except permitting a pet off-leash.

I lost my usual confident aura and felt the need to hide a part of myself from many of the friends and colleagues I had been so close with before. The event had served to place my identity on unsolid ground. My friends and family members had always classified myself as a dependable, reliable, and moral person. I had a good work ethic, a faithful disposition, and a lighthearted laugh, which I used often. But now, after having my humanity questioned and my body physically confined without a valid reason, all those previous characteristics I was known for seemed to lift up and away from me as I reached to catch and hold them close. I felt the need in my career and at my church home to continually prove my worth, my goodness, and my integrity to myself first.

Nevertheless, my spirit grew stronger and more resilient as I continued to cultivate career opportunities, healthy friendships, and a nourishing lifestyle. After graduating against all odds with my Ph.D. in History from Temple University, I resisted the temptation to fall dormant and sought a new opportunity for learning. I decided to move into financial planning and began studying for all my required tests. After passing all three and acquiring my license, I found a position working beneath a broker-dealer in 2007. In order to secure this job, my employer would need to run a background check on me by running my fingerprints through Live Scan.

Considering all my penalties had been served faithfully without issue, I was under the impression that the charge filed against me following the park fiasco in 2004 would no longer be present on my government record. Yet after running my fingerprints, my employer informed me that he had encountered an issue during my background check, "LAM- Unlaw Exposure of Body in Public." Now, I am a prostitute?! I immediately informed him that I had no criminal record and even fully disclosed the circumstances of my previous case. Thankfully the broker believed me and followed the necessary protocols for securing my status with his company. He wrote the court to subpoena all documents under my name, and they came back clear with only the transcripts from my visits to Hollywood court, it came back with just the dog off leash.

While this was both humiliating and frustrating, I never suspected that this obstacle involved anything other than the dog park incident. I enjoyed working in this new field and filed the occurrence away

CHAPTER THREE: A "CLERICAL ERROR"

without a second thought. I only wondered if I'd have to disclose the same information to each new employer for the rest of my life, despite being promised that my record would be fully expunged. Onward and upward, right?

Wrong. The very next step forward I would take in my career would prove to have the very same obstacles. In 2010, I began courting a new opportunity with the U.S. Department of Commerce. As soon as it was professionally appropriate to do so, I sat down with the hiring agent and disclosed my 2004 run-in with the legislative system. I explained the circumstances and alerted him that this information, "dog off leash" would come back on my record when the department ran its background check. I chose to focus less on the shame of the interaction and more on my newfound self-advocacy. I felt empowered by my professionalism in the face of adversity. I hoped that my new employer would see my honesty and understand the irrelevance of the situation to my job performance. They did, and I began putting my decade of continuous education in political science, history, and finance to use in this job that encapsulated all my interests and satisfied my ambition.

In 2011, I was set to take a business trip to China. I was now the high profile Regional Partnership Specialist within the Department of Commerce and had an important meeting that I needed time to prepare for on-site. I was also due for a renewal of my government clearance, which was granted every 90 days. I took a flight from Los Angeles to Vancouver, Canada, and settled in for a layover. When it came time for me to board my connecting flight to China, the airport security staff began to ask questions. Remaining calm, I handed over my federal identification card, my passport, and my driver's license. I answered all questions confidently and felt sure that I would soon be cleared and allowed to continue on with my trip. I worked directly beneath the President of the United States and figured that America's highest level of security clearance would certainly grant me access to board a plane in Canada.

Not so. They sent me back on a flight to Los Angeles. Enraged and past my patience limit, I immediately walked back into the Hollywood courthouse and demanded to see every shred of paper that involved me in any way. I needed to know exactly what it was that my employers and the airport security staff were seeing. I needed to know exactly why a nonviolent offense, which was completely unfounded in the first place, was impeding my ability to complete my assigned job tasks and making me appear unprofessional in the meantime.

It had been seven years since I unclipped Nna from his leash at Griffith Park. Though his breed was specified as a "red nose pitbull terrier" on his adoption papers, his muzzle was quite gray at this point and had been for a while. My beloved dog was aging into his senior years while I continued to pay the social and occupational consequences of taking an evening hike a lifetime ago. Even so, I had done my time and paid the unwarranted consequences. Frankly, I was fed up.

When I received my records from the courthouse clerk, I only saw the same information regarding my 2004 dog off leash. Exactly as I suspected. Armed with this paperwork, I again booked a flight to Vancouver. At the terminal once again, staving off the eerie feeling of deja vu, I presented my information to the security staff.

"Yes," they said, "that's fine. But there's something the government has placed here under your name."

Befuddled, I began to ask questions. "I don't understand. I work for the U.S. government."

I felt as though I'd swum across an ocean only to be captured on the shore. If I wasn't trusted to fly on a Canadian airline, how could I be trusted to handle confidential information and government budgets? In much the same way that I had been on those sandy rocks amidst the brush at Griffith Park, I stood confused on the flat blue carpet of the foreign airport customs checkpoint. I couldn't seem to catch a break.

I made some calls to investigate what exact issue I had run into in Vancouver. I needed to have full travel clearance in order to continue fulfilling my current role. I was told that America's immigration system and requirements do not align with Canada's and that the two countries had regulatory disagreements about admitting travelers onto international flights. So, when I had attempted to move through

CHAPTER THREE: A "CLERICAL ERROR"

customs as an employee of the American government, the Canadian customs officers had detained me and denied my admission. Once the onus lifted from me and my fabricated criminal record and landed squarely on some petty international dispute, my academic interest was piqued, and my anger subsided. I completed my business in China uneventfully and headed back to L.A. and my normal life. It hadn't been my fault. Next time I wanted to travel internationally, I'd schedule my layover somewhere else. No big deal.

My contract was renewed three times as I continued my work in the department. That is until one end-of-year checkpoint when I was unexpectedly informed that my contract would not be renewed. I was surprised. I had received positive performance reviews, delivered exceptional work, and had good relationships with the others on my team. I had recently been receiving significant positive media attention for the work I completed on behalf of the current administration. I had even been featured on CNN. I couldn't seem to connect the dots between my objectively beneficial contributions to the department and their decision not to renew my contract. I respectfully inquired why I wouldn't be staying on, but no one would tell me anything. I was beginning to feel crazy. Was I on some sort of blacklist?

Whether I received an explanation or not, I'd need to find another source of income, and fast. Since working for other people had proven to be unpredictable, I tried my hand at working for myself again. I started my own marketing organization with the intention to continue the work that had garnered so much attention during my time with the Department of Commerce but ended up gaining my first organic client within a year. As a Subcontractor we would be handling, outreach and marketing strategies and materials for the new California High-Speed Rail. I was ecstatic and buzzing with gratitude. I felt such satisfaction, knowing that I could fend for myself using my God-given skills, education, and talent. I had even paid tribute to my faith by naming my business A-Selah. And of course, amidst all these swirling positive feelings, my team and I got down to business to make sure our client was satisfied.

Suddenly, without explanation, I received a notification from the rail system's liaison that they would no longer be in need of my services. My life was beginning to feel a bit like Groundhog Day. I was on a path of rugs, and they all kept being yanked from beneath my feet one after the other. I was once again provided no background information as to why the client discontinued our working relationship. Ironically, we had been working on outreach to hire local labor for this avant-garde transportation system, and I found myself once again out of a job. I knew they still needed marketing, so it wasn't a matter of demand. And we had successfully hired over 900,000 employees nationwide, stacking the cause to the brim with valuable talent. Something was going on behind the scenes that no one would tell me about.

The only common denominator in this sequence of professional disappointments was me, so I knew that the withdrawal of contract was based on something I had done. I felt like I had hit another dead end in a maze chock full of them. I apologized to my staff and went back to the drawing board—after all, I still had bills to pay. While I searched for jobs, my company phone line continued to ring. People were still calling A-Selah to look for employment with the new high-speed rail. Shame burned red in my throat as I served the same one-liner hundreds of times.

"Sorry, but we're no longer working on that project." Click.

As I gathered myself and scoured for resources to give me a leg up in the professional world, my reservoir of savings slowly began to dwindle. Between long bouts of depression and anger, I'd be struck with the bizarre humor of it all. I kept waiting for someone to pop out from behind the bushes with a camera to reveal that I was being pranked. In a matter of months, I had gone from speaking on a reputable news channel in thousands of American homes to scraping the bottom of my savings barrel to pay my mortgage. I was running out of money and soon began receiving courtesy notices about my home's impending foreclosure. I needed to figure something out quickly.

In the years between my false imprisonment and my professional demise, I had purchased a large two-story home. As my financial security dwindled to nothing, my neighbor had approached me with a suggestion I did not take up immediately nor did I make the decision lightly but now, I needed to look closely into it. "Your home is so big for just one," she remarked. "Why don't you consider fostering children? You have rooms for them to stay in and a heart for service. And the government will assist you with funding to take care of them."

It wasn't a bad idea at all. Though this spiritual tribulation was the most brutal I had experienced by far, I looked back on my life and realized that placing myself in service to others had always been a gentle salve for whatever wounds I was nursing at the time. Helping others reminded me that my own troubles were so small compared to the vast expanse of souls wandering the earth, and so trivial compared to the mighty flood of God's everlasting love. At a time when I felt like I didn't have much to offer the world, I had this spacious home. I decided to fill my empty spaces with children who could benefit from my care and mentorship.

I was unmarried with Nna as my primary companion, so I knew I wouldn't be interested in fostering to adopt. Instead, I wanted to use my space as a small-scale transitional home, a safe space for children in the system. I knew I could provide a haven of consistency and generosity for young people who were living tumultuous lives of betrayal, neglect, and abuse. I needed to channel all my sorrow and confusion into something wholesome and bright. So in 2011, I qualified through Child Protective Services as a suitable foster parent and opened my doors in a spirit of hope.

The Story of Job

As untimely as it may seem, I need to pause here in medias res—in the middle of things—and bring wisdom to what I believe was occurring below the surface of my life at this time. While the outward circumstances of my 2004 blunder are important and merit continued conversation about the flaws in America's justice system, they don't fully represent my experience. As my life turned upside down and misfortunes repeatedly befell me, I continually turned to my faith and spirituality. I searched for understanding through prayer and communion with my savior.

In the Bible, there's an entire book in the Old Testament devoted to telling the story of how a man named Job lost everything good in his life. In it, Job begins as a highly favored child of God. He has a loving family, a happy marriage, a fertile plot of land occupied by cattle, a healthy body, and considerable wealth. Meanwhile, in the cosmos, God remarks to Satan about Job's righteousness, to which Satan offers an interesting rebuttal. Satan claims that Job's unshakeable faith and virtue are only a symptom of his abundantly blessed life. Satan claims that if Job were to face calamity or disaster, he would immediately turn against God and obey only himself. God, confident in Job's loyalty, grants Satan permission to test him. The only rule is that Satan cannot take Job's life in the process.

And so it begins. On the first day after this ethereal agreement, Job receives word from four separate messengers that all of his livestock, children, and servants have died due to hand-to-hand violence or natural disasters. In sorrow, he shaves his head, dresses in rags, and begins to cry out to God in mourning.

Not long after this, Job is stricken with painful lesions all over his body. They are so excruciating that his wife, a witness to his torture, suggests that Job abandon his faith, curse God, and go on about his merry way. Job resists this temptation and continues praying and supplicating with the Holy Spirit as his sickness drags on. Shocked by his wife's suggestions that he abandon his spiritual truth, Job sends his wife away. Bereft by the loss of their children and the scorn of her husband, Job's wife goes away to live among the cattle, where she eventually dies.

When four of Job's friends come to visit his sickbed, they engage in a long philosophical debate about the nature of God and humankind. They inform Job that he must be suffering retribution for some spiritual misstep, even suggesting at one point that his incessant talking has warranted this series of personal tragedies. Job refuses to accept this belief and once again stands firm in his faith.

After losing his family, wealth, health, and reputation, Job maintains his allegiance to God. He has passed the test. Back in heaven, God finally calls Satan off Job's case now that he has proven his unconditional alignment with the Lord. Satan skulks away to do evil elsewhere, and God restores Job's blessings, offering him new wealth, a new wife, a healed body, and ten more vibrant children.

My story has thus far been overrun with misfortune and pain, and I'm here to tell you that things will only get worse. To me, however, the spiritual warfare that was unfolding within my own heart carries more weight than the self-serving choices of a flawed human governance. As I continued to lose my wealth and reputation inexplicably, I saw the parallels between my challenges and Job's. I resolved myself to stay faithful at all costs. My life before had been abundantly blessed, just like Job's. I had literally been living my dream. I knew that while I was down on Earth fighting for myself and my home, the Lord was in heaven fighting right alongside me.

Nna's Death

My third and fourth foster intakes were a pair of teenage sisters who hailed from a long life of unthinkable abuse. I brought them into my home and introduced them to a stable life and routine, including assigned household chores, weekly Bible studies, and church on Sundays. And of course, there was Nna all along, wagging and lolling his tongue and generally delighting in our newly busy household. As always, I was his number one priority, but that didn't stop him from developing attachments to his new temporary sisters.

My style of parenting placed special emphasis on the importance of boundaries and empathy. While I made my priorities, intentions, and expectations clear, I also refrained from projecting unreasonable restrictions on the lives of these two young ladies. They knew that I expected teamwork inside the home, and they knew that I believed in God and would encourage them to listen to the gospel as long as they resided in my home. Still, if one of the girls communicated that she was tired, afraid, or too overwhelmed to perform her usual duties or join me for church events, I would offer her the benefit of the doubt and allow her to take restful time alone.

The two girls had another sister who had already aged out of the system but lived locally. This sister and the older of the two in my home were transfixed with gore, horror, and dark magic. I often saw things such as spellbooks, crystals, and other paraphernalia lying around the house. It wasn't a strange occurrence to hear non-English chanting come out of the older girl's room. I chalked this up as the result of a trauma-filled life. I knew that children who had been hurt this badly often put up a hard exterior in order to cope or even had an obsession with violence born out of what had happened to them. I often felt unnerved by the 17-year-old girl's attraction to spiritual darkness but kept the light of hope burning in my heart for her as I continued to pray for her life and expose her to God's love.

In the meantime, I made sure to offer her understanding and compassion for the entirety of her stay in my care. So when she asked whether I'd allow her older sister to spend the weekend in our home one day, I said yes. I wanted her to be able to maintain the few family connections she had remaining in her life. That Saturday, about midnight and what pop culture calls, "demon-time" as I was working late, when I began to hear chanting from the older girl's room where she was spending time with her sister, I was startled. I knew that this was a part of the girl's personal spirituality and knew better than to disallow her from having her own beliefs, but I also felt uncomfortable with the menacing tones of their voices as they used a room in my home for pagan practices. Even so, I continued with my work and tried to zone them out.

The weekend concluded without any further abnormalities, and before we knew it, it was time for Wednesday Bible study, which we usually attended as a group. That day, though, the older girl asked if she could stay in and catch up on sleep after staying up late all weekend with her visitor. I didn't see a reason to refuse her this, so I allowed it. We had been in an argument earlier that day about chores, and I figured she and I could use some space apart at that time anyway, as the girl seemed to still be angry about my expectations for her participation in keeping our home clean.

When I arrived home from church, Nna ran up to me, breathing heavily and seeming very upset. Alarmed, I knelt to his level and spoke in calming tones while petting his head. I figured he just hadn't been let out to potty for a long time and needed to relieve himself. Business proceeded as usual that night, and we all tucked safely into our beds for a night of sleep. Nna took his position on the dog bed in my room. I enjoyed only a few hours of sleep before waking up to see that Nna was sitting in a puddle of his own upchucked blood. He was breathing heavily and unable to move. I looked at the mess and saw that there were fleshy bits in his vomit. I would later find out at the vet's office that this was a part of his liver.

The younger of the two sisters heard the commotion and woke up to see what was the matter. She helped me clean the blood and waited through the night with me to keep Nna awake until the vet's office opened. In the worst possible timing, while I was gathering my things at daybreak to take Nna for medical treatment, I heard a knock at the front door. It was a CPS agent.

"Hi!" she said cheerily, "I'm here to perform a drop-in home visit."

"I'm sorry, but I'm having an emergency right now." I beseeched her, "Now is not a good time."

The agent began shouldering her way through the door, refusing to hear me or, perhaps, to believe me. I allowed her through into the foyer and continued to explain my present circumstances. I was interrupted by the older foster child as she made her way down the stairs.

"*Didn't you hear her?!*" She spat at the agent, "We're having an emergency. She needs to go. *You* need to go."

Miraculously, the agent bent to the teenager's will in an instant. She apologized for the inconvenience and abruptly walked back to her car. I turned to look at the child in disbelief. Her facial expression showed no surprise or distress. At that very moment, Nna, who had been inches from death and completely immobile for the entire night, muscled himself up and pulled his body in front of mine as though to protect me from her. It was as if a fire alarm began ringing there between my ears. Something wasn't right.

"Nna is hurt. He threw up blood. Chunks of clots in the blood. We're going to the vet to see what's wrong," I explained, assuming the girl was uninformed about the current situation.

"I'm going with her," the little sister said, "Do you want to come?"

"No," the older sister said firmly, "I'll stay here to clean up the blood."

The gears in my mind switched into overdrive as we made our way to the vet's office. I felt a pit in my stomach. I am not sure how I can be so calm. Why I was so calm, while my beloved Nna was dying. I was responsible for bringing into our lives the person who was responsible for his soon to be demise. But wisdom had taken over. She was in charge of us all now.

There I found out that the damage to Nna's internal organs was far too extensive. I caressed his graying head as the veterinarian put my best friend of 14 years to sleep. I wept. The only constant source of joy and connection in my life for over a decade was now gone less than a second. As I drove home with my foster child in the passenger seat, she spoke in a trembling voice: "My sister needs help," she said. "I didn't know how bad it was until now, but...she did it." Of course, she was confessing to me that her sister had done it.

"I know," I said.

That's the thing about me. I was blessed with an impossibly accurate intuition. Truthfully, I've been blessed with the spiritual gift of prophecy. A Seer. That morning between 12am and 3:11am, something had taken place in the spiritual realm and the aftermath was what we were now dealing with. And that sharp instinct of mine was tugging at me, hinting to me that there was something more to the recurrent mishaps of my life than just bad luck. Something wasn't right and in our meeting with the social workers, she partly confessed, "She is too good. She knows who I am." The conference room at the Department of Children Services became unbearably cold. We both knew who each other were even if most in the room were clueless and confused by her statement.

I continued to navigate my new role as a foster parent while relying on my sturdy work ethic to open more professional doors. In 2013, Goldman Sachs invited me to participate in their 10,000 Small Businesses Program as the program manager. Of course, I accepted, both relieved to land a dependable income and ecstatic to be involved with such a successful company. Yet once again, when my Live Scan background check went through, the job offer was rescinded without explanation. That helpless feeling returned.

Once again, I marveled at the impact that one harmless park violation could have on a person's life. I was incredulous but chalked the whole situation up to a markedly dysfunctional justice system. There was nothing to do but persist. I couldn't roll over and allow my life to slip away. My efforts soon landed me a job appointment from UCLA as their potential new pathology lab manager. As a lifelong proponent and participant in academic spheres, I had high hopes for this new opportunity. I was in communication with the hiring manager to complete all necessary paperwork and begin work, but he mysteriously became unresponsive and nonspecific at some point during our dealings. Mere weeks later, I received a letter from the university indicating that they had decided to appoint someone else.

I cried, fasted, and prayed. I felt that my only option was to create a unique opportunity for myself. Working for other entities just wasn't working out. I decided that I'd open an actual home for children with disabilities. While working out the logistics to accomplish this goal, I reached out to California Mentors to begin gaining experience and immersing myself in this particular type of service. That's when I received a call from their offices and received the following alarming question from the hiring manager:

"Doctor, why didn't you tell us that you had a criminal record?"

I scheduled a meeting with her to see exactly which documents were informing her of my supposed criminal record. This was my opportunity to get a look at what all these employers had seen. I would finally know what had landed me on the blacklist. I thanked the Lord for this cooperative and communicative administrator and, a couple of weeks later, walked into her office. There I saw, on a document watermarked as coming from the Californian Department of Justice, the following words:

> ***This person has a criminal record. This person cannot be near any clients.***

I immediately asked to make a copy of the document, and the hiring agent complied.

Within days, I marched back into Hollywood court, which was soon becoming my least favorite building on the planet, presented the file, and demanded again to see every single piece of information that fell under my name. They sent me to one of the back rooms, where clerks sat typing in their cubicles. I once again requested my criminal record. The clerks treated me with haughtiness and disdain. If facial expressions could be translated, theirs would have said, "It's *your* criminal record. Shouldn't you know?" But I didn't know. And I desperately needed to.

As I struggled to break the red tape with these courthouse clerks, a young lawyer looked on curiously. He saw what transpired between us and how upset I appeared. He pulled me aside to ask me what was wrong. I explained the situation and scheduled a meeting with him. At our meeting, I handed over all my paperwork. He began running my identification numbers through his computer and nodded unsurprisingly at the charge of permitting a pet off a leash.

Then, he asked me a question I would never forget. "Who is Patricia Jackson?"

There were two different case numbers attached to my dog park case as though related. They were both felonies registered under the name Patricia Jackson. While I had been suffering through the worst professional drought of my life and praying for jobs to rain down, a certain Patricia Jackson was accruing federal charges for drug abuse, prostitution, and robbery. And the government had been placing them under my identification number.

The California state government had stolen my identity. When I returned to the courthouse to ask about this death sentence, they denied it but I continued with my query with the intent and posture to never let anyone have peace until I get the truth. Almost dismissing me, I was given one laughably simple explanation.

"It must have been a clerical error."

CHAPTER SUMMARY

- I complete my probation and community service and pay my fees
- I am mysteriously stonewalled by several employers in a row.

CHAPTER THREE: A "CLERICAL ERROR"

- I start my own business, A-Selah.
- I become a certified foster parent.
- Nna, my beloved dog, is poisoned and dies.
- I discover that two felonies are classified onto my criminal record, though I never committed any.

In the next chapter, you will learn about the steps I took to advocate for myself and clear my name.

CHAPTER FOUR: THE FIGHT

Every single job that I had applied to since 2004 had been seeing these words associated with my name. Drug abuse. Prostitution. Robbery. Possession. Endangerment. My criminal record, which should not have existed whatsoever, was a convoluted document that carried with it two names and multiple felonies. But since my prospective employers weren't lawyers or sleuths, they didn't see the peculiarity of the two ethnically disparate names, nor did they see the dichotomy between my qualifications and Patricia Jackson's. All my employers had seen was drama, darkness, immorality, and unsavory character tacked onto my paper trail. All they had seen was a sloppy stain on my reputation that would transfer onto theirs should they hire me.

I didn't blame anyone for choosing a different avenue than hiring a felon. I blamed the government. Whether they had been careless or malicious in committing this oversight didn't matter to me, because, at the end of the day, it had ruined my life. For over ten years, I had been paying another person's debt to society, and the cost was astronomical.

Truthfully, I don't know how any of it happened. To this day, I don't know who Patricia Jackson is or how she and I became entangled in the filing cabinets of California's Department of Justice. I hope that she's well. I'm certainly not.

CHAPTER FOUR: THE FIGHT

On that day in 2014, I wasn't okay either. The kind-hearted lawyer who had seen me struggling with the courthouse clerks earlier in the day had taken his own personal time to not only print my entire record but also wait in a long dreary line to receive an official government seal on the document. We stood in the echoing hallway of the courthouse, and he passed an envelope into my hands as though we were exchanging gold.

"Whatever you do, do not lose this. I've made another copy, but this one is yours. Keep this safe, because you're going to need it."

The implication in his somber tone informed me that this battle wouldn't be an easy one. I knew, just by the composure of his clouding eyes, that I wouldn't be granted some magical get-out-of-jail-free card. The information that I held between my two fingers was proof that the government itself had committed a crime against me, a layperson. They wouldn't take this information kindly. That much I knew for sure.

I scheduled a hearing with the judge as soon as I possibly could, which was still two months away from the day I first saw Patricia Jackson's name. Though it's typical for legislative issues to take months or even years to reach a conclusion, the interim can be brutal for people like me. My homeowner status was hanging on by a thread as I continued to receive alerts from the bank about my impending foreclosure. I didn't have any hopeful job prospects. I sat on the cushion of my savings and ambition and tried my best to balance my dwindling financial resources with the privileged lifestyle I had been accustomed to. It was the strangest sensation to run in the same social circles with millionaires while secretly searching for humble apartments in preparation for my impending home foreclosure. For a person on the brink of financial collapse and homelessness, a judge's stacked schedule can feel like a death sentence. If it weren't for the favor and protection of my Holy Spirit, I might have lost everything before I even had my day in court. Red tape isn't just an annoyance. For some, it's the last nail in a coffin.

When the judge finally was able to lend me his ear, I let my sealed document do the talking. There were no name changes on my record. My name was then and had always been OnyekamBuashie Amatokwu.

Fate had offered me a glorious respite by granting me a name with undeniable African heritage and an inimitable lineup of vowels and consonants. The only other person I had met with my name was the woman who had given it to me—my grandmother, the Queen Mother. Placed side by side with Patricia Jackson's Anglo-Saxon moniker, the judge, blinked and his eyes widened as he looked up at me and the kind attorney, he couldn't deny that there had been a deadly mixup.

I stood on the courtroom's thin carpet as the judge looked over his glasses at my record. His eyebrows arched and lifted in disbelief, and for the first time ever, the light of common sense broke through the windows of a publicly funded building. "This isn't right," he said matter of factly.

Immediately, I was granted a full expungement of my record. This was good news, but wouldn't occur immediately. In this upside-down world of madness that had been created for me by the state of California, I still needed to make an appointment to have my fingerprints taken to prove that I wasn't Patricia Jackson. Once again, not once but it took two appointments to be set for months away. Why? you ask. I later learned that they were trying to buy time, or waste time. The government and the court didn't want to be held liable for damages done to me. Before the journey to a cleared name had even begun, I foresaw the difficulties I'd inevitably face. I didn't need a job a year from now. I need one immediately. I needed to be off the blacklist and onto someone's payroll, preferably in a position that used my degrees.

I explained this to the judge. I couldn't walk out those heavy oak doors without putting words to my sorrow.

"Sir, thank you for the expungement," I said sincerely. "But I need help now. I haven't been able to get a job because of this. My house will be foreclosed upon before the year's end if I can't find a way to make money. I just accepted a job offer, and if this shows up on my background check when they run it, which will be soon, then I will be excluded from a six-figure income and gainful employment that could help restore my assets to balance. If I can't get this off my record, I'm going to be on the streets."

I could see genuine hurt in the man's eyes as he sat in his robes behind the podium, but the checks and balances of the powers that be wouldn't allow him to set me free. "I'm so sorry," he expressed, "this is all I can do. You need to file a legal claim against the state of California for this. This shouldn't have happened to you."

I left the courthouse that day with my only weapon tucked under my arm—a manila folder that held proof of my innocence. Before I was able to roll my fingers in black ink and press them onto watermarked grid paper, proving the whorls and lines in my fingertips didn't belong to any Patricia Jackson, my home foreclosed and I became homeless. The job I had on the line during my hearing had been the UCLA-appointed position as pathology lab manager, which was lost due to the obsolete felony charges under my name. At first, I had only been interested in doing what it took to regain my professional status as a hireable, valuably skilled employee. But now that I knew why it all had happened and presently felt the worst of all consequences thus far —homelessness—I resolved to see justice served. I wouldn't just take the bare minimum of a record expungement. I would find out who placed these charges under my name in error, who had allowed them to stay there, and who had hidden them from me while my life fell in shambles around my feet for the last ten years. I would find every culpable party and draw the truth of this matter to the surface. I was raised to see the worth in my own eyes. I was raised to demand respect, and I had done all the work necessary to deserve it. I wasn't some nobody who could be falsely imprisoned and nonchalantly blacklisted by a house of unconstitutional cards.

I was going to fight my case in honor of every racial profiling victim who is lost in a vortex of paper shuffling, postponed appointments, pushbacks, and unreasonable requirements. For every person who hears myths of American freedom, democracy, and endless opportunity and feels as though they're listening to a fairytale fantasy. For those who couldn't afford to fight for themselves after being drained of resources by a cold, senseless bureaucracy, I would fight. I will always fight because the battle now is the Lord fighting though me.

The question now was where to start. I had nothing. Months after that first productive hearing, I received Judicial Clearance from one of Patricia Jackson's felonies only to discover as I stated earlier that I'd need to repeat the process to receive it for the second. I sat through pitiless L.A. traffic and sweated through countless pantsuits on behalf of someone else's mistake. I felt robbed of all dignity each time I heard the click of my heels on that government building's beige tiles. In the real world, when one person makes a mistake that harms another, the perpetrator is the one who must run the rat race to receive forgiveness. In the world of government, especially when the government itself is in the wrong, the victim is the one who must bend over backward to earn an apology. I laugh when I hear others call this "public service." It couldn't be further from the truth.

To be clear, Patricia Jackson knew as much about me as I knew about her. While she may have been guilty of committing crimes, she did not steal my identity. In fact, at the time that the two felonies placed on my record had supposedly been committed, Ms. Jackson had been incarcerated. There was never any question or attempt to pin this mistake on her. It had been clear from the beginning that a government worker, or maybe a group of them along the way, had stolen my government-issued identification number and used it to process another citizen's crimes. The state government had stolen my identity after falsely imprisoning and penalizing me for a minor park violation, and I'm being generous to even call it that.

As the months wore on and I sought temporary housing with a kind church member and friend Shelly Paul for close to two months then as a renter, it never once occurred to me that I was being duped. Even after all this trickery, I truly believed each monotonous receptionist's voice and facial expressions when they said that the earliest available appointments were months from right now. I believed that this was just the nature of official problem-solving. I didn't realize that a statute of limitations had come into play the moment I discovered a crime had been committed against me. Under state law, I had exactly one year from the date that I discovered what had happened to me to file a damages claim. I didn't realize that my opponent, who knew the nuances of the Establishment's game so well, was intentionally slowing my progress so that the statute would expire before I was able to file my official complaint. I couldn't file a damages claim until my record had been fully expunged, and both Patricia Jackson's felonies had been cleared from my file. And I couldn't gain judicial clearance until Judge or Attorney So-and-so had an opening in his calendar. The manipulation was subtle and venomous.

Much like a basketball player dribbling lazily at half court with five seconds left in the game, the department of justice was waiting me out and running the clock down. They were counting on me to lack the intelligence and diligence to beat them at their own game. I cannot imagine how many times this tactic has succeeded, but God didn't let it win against me. Later I would discover that, had I not scheduled my fingerprinting appointment on the same day that I'd had the first hearing, I would have easily been left behind in the dust of a forfeited lawsuit. I would never have been able to soar over all the hurdles the system had placed in front of me within my allotted 12 months. But, stubborn and smart as I am, God did through me. Here's how.

I acted immediately on each new piece of information. I kept my eyes on the prize: a clean criminal record. With each injustice, there are a hundred smaller ones in the day-to-day dealings of the court. For example, I shouldn't have had to gain two judicial clearances. This was a delaying tactic. But had I chosen to lawyer up and fight this smaller unfairness, I would have missed my opportunity to file my damages claim within the allotted time. I always said that Google is set up to spy on folks but the devil can be used to my advantage. Each time that I showed up in the courthouse, I was fully prepared. I refused to be caught up on any technicality. I kept proof of residence, identification, social security card, and all other necessary information on my person each time I handled official matters. I educated myself. I never stopped being my own biggest advocate. Even after hiring lawyers or running into others who seemed as though they wanted to help me, discernment and wisdom I didn't allow me to pass the baton. This was my battle, and I knew that no one was better equipped or more invested than I was to see it through.

The kind lawyer who had used his access to government records to finally inform me of the errors on my file had done it purely as a good deed. I did not end up paying for his services, as I had naively expected in the beginning that the court would be exceedingly apologetic for the harmful blunder and would make reparations immediately. When it became clear to me that this would be no easy fix, I hired a new lawyer, H. Foxy. Yes, Foxy! The name is always an indication and I should have been wise as a serpent but I maintained my dove stance. I needed to believe that there were still more good people left in this profession. Upon our first meeting, his Foxy's eyes shone with the glee of a surefire victory. The details of my case were so clean-cut and indisputable that he must have known I'd tuck another courthouse win under his belt.

Unfortunately, even in a country that regulates effective legal counsel for each citizen, loyalties still tend to lie with the most powerful opponent. I, living off of savings and watching my social, professional, and financial security slowly drain away, was not the most powerful opponent. The district attorney was.

We've all been in romantic relationships where our partner begins to slowly distance themselves emotionally. Suddenly compliments become rare, physical affection tapers off, and there is no such thing as a direct answer. I had endured this suspicious behavior many times from men here and there, and I knew better than to cling on tighter to a person dead set on slipping my grip. Nevertheless, I was not prepared to experience this dynamic with my own hired attorney. What had been an exciting opportunity mere weeks earlier now seemed to be a nuisance to my lawyer as we continued exchanging emails, calls, and paperwork. One day, my lawyer asked me to remove the names of the park ranger who had racially profiled me, the police officers who had falsely imprisoned me, and the most unprofessional, tacky and wicked public defender ever, Patricia Hudges who had failed to fight for my best interests from my formal complaint. I can say so much more maltreatment I endured at the hands of Patricia Hudges, this "public defender" who knew I was innocent yet, she held the smoking gun and did not have any problem pulling it on an innocent person. She is the "public defender" yet I was not human to her but another young African American without a future worth fighting for. I still attempted to speak with her about the now missing recordings that once proved my innocence ten years ago. Her rebuttal to my question was, "what, are you still on probation? Why are you here making demands?' In my mind's eye, I saw a waving bright red flag.

CHAPTER FOUR: THE FIGHT

If I hadn't been unlawfully detained by a prejudiced park ranger and falsely imprisoned for letting my dog off-leash, I would have had no prior run-ins with the law. My name would not have been floating around in the woefully disorganized files of the state's legislative branch. Patricia Jackson's felonies would not have been errantly ascribed to my identification number, and I wouldn't have lost all footing on my career path. My home wouldn't have been foreclosed upon. No aspect of my story was mutually exclusive from the next—they all worked together to leave me destitute. My ethics and my passion for finding justice would not allow me to remove the names of those who had allowed this to happen. And, in practical terms, I had no idea who had actually been responsible for tainting my identity and why? I still didn't know if this had been done willfully or ignorantly but I am now leaning on the latter. Any one of those people I had run into during my many court visits could have been involved. I wanted each one of them to stay present on my file in binding black and white print.

To my lawyer's H. Foxy's request, I offered a resounding "No. I can't do that. Until I get a proper trial, everyone stays."

Before my attorney made his subtle shift from gung-ho defender to double-sided placater, he himself had advised me as such. Truthfully, I was only spouting off to him at that moment what he had said to me on many occasions. I was dumbstruck by his ability to contradict himself so directly and, at the same time, incensed by his failure to offer effective counsel. If anyone knew my financial situation, it was my lawyer. Yet I had paid his retaining fee and for every single hour of his time. While my money sat heavy in his pockets, he advised me to render my own argument useless. Once again, I suspected some backroom dealings had gone on between the last time I met with him and our present conversation. The department of justice must have bribed or threatened him in some way to make my case disappear. Now more than ever, I was acutely aware of my aloneness in this fight.

Still, I was all too conscious of my lack of training in legal matters. I needed a lawyer to help me get through all the thick, convoluted language of my documents. I needed a professional to help me navigate the intricacies of the court. So I kept my alignment with this person. About 90 days before the one-year statute of limitations expired, my lawyer and I had reached the final drafting stage of filing my formal damages claim. Week after week, he'd call me to request an extension on submitting the claim. Week after week, I believed that he was working hard and granted him extra time. Finally, when he had exhausted all possible extension opportunities for drafting the complaint, my lawyer called me up to tell me that he would be recusing himself from my case. It was Thanksgiving weekend, and I was surrounded by friends and family. My case brief was due for filing within the next week.

Infuriated and utterly shocked, I refused to let him hang up. "This is illegal!" I shouted. "You cannot just leave your client a week before the briefing. What am I supposed to do now?!" I was asking myself this question just as much as I was asking him. Neither of us had an answer. My now ex-lawyer offered nothing but a lukewarm apology and ended the phone call with, "it is to your best interest to drop the case." For the remainder of the holiday weekend, I struggled to keep my head above the waters of depression and helplessness. I would not give myself the permission to fall apart. Once everyone had gone home and life resumed that following Monday, I waited to hear from the courts whether they'd be granting my attorney his request for recusal. I wanted to take solace in my knowledge that this sort of last-minute withdrawal was fully against the law, but after years of disappointments and betrayals, I knew better than to trust anything one hundred percent. Sure enough, I received the news that my attorney would be allowed to absolve himself of all responsibility regarding myself and my case. Just when I thought nothing could surprise me anymore, I watched the legal system break its own laws once again. I felt as though the wind had been knocked out of my chest but I had to remind myself that this battle was not mine to fight even if I was feeling all the blows landing one after the other.

As soon as I possibly could, I visited the courts to ask for an extension to submit the opening brief considering my special circumstances. According to state law, my attorney was required to give me a grace period between losing his services and finding those of another legal professional. Since he had not done so, I felt that it would only be reasonable for the judge to offer me more time. Of course, this request was denied.

As much as I wanted to assume the fetal position and spend the week licking my emotional wounds, I knew that I had no other option but to buckle down, open my laptop, grab a ballpoint pen and get to work. I knew that I'd be filing my own legal claim that week, and I had practically no time at all to do it. Naturally, I contacted the attorney one last time to retrieve the documents related to my case. With indifference, he told me he'd send them to me via mail. This was exceedingly frustrating, considering I had mere days before my filing deadline, and America's postal system is called snail mail for a reason. Knowing he had no allegiance to me whatsoever, I accepted this unsatisfactory answer and nervously awaited the mail truck. It never came. I returned to the courthouse downtown to request *their* copies of my documents. They told me that they had destroyed everything pertaining to my case during the process of closing down the old court building in Hollywood. Also, my case is over ten years old. Everything had been erased.

As a last-ditch effort, I contacted that public defender who had disillusioned me a decade earlier during my dog park case hearings. We met in person soon after, and I asked her whether she had any documents in her possession that might be pertinent to my ongoing efforts. Rather than offering assistance or answering my question, she began questioning me. "What other crimes have you committed?" She asked impudently. "If you haven't committed any felonies, you shouldn't need any files to prove it." My mouth hung open in disbelief as she continued projecting uninformed assumptions and unsolicited opinions onto me without knowing the context of my situation. I was absolutely livid. No matter where I turned, I saw a hostile face. Forget help; I couldn't even find anyone who wasn't actively working against me.

"Wow," I almost whispered back with chilling composure, "ma'am, you are one of many people who have worked together in ruining my life. And you cannot even grant me the dignity of checking your files without contempt?" I knew that I shouldn't stay in conversation with this attorney for much longer, else I'd likely lose the composure I was working so hard to maintain. I concluded the conversation hastily and walked away.

My documents were destroyed. I felt like I'd just been asked to run a marathon on the spot without any prior training. I had no support, no crutches, no foundational bank of knowledge from which to build my case brief. I had been spurned, kicked, and left bare. Luckily, I had sent two copies of my original case file, the one that the kind-hearted attorney had printed and sealed, to two trusted friends earlier in the year. Once I saw the clerical stunts that the courthouse kept pulling, I knew I'd need to increase my odds of survival by maintaining a paper trail. I contacted these two confidants and retrieved the original proof of wrongdoing. Running only on fumes and faith, I settled in for an endurance test of massive proportions. I had two days left to write my own case brief.

With my glasses on and about a hundred tabs open on my computer, I got to work with the help from my cousin, Etabuno. The tail end of my pen flew and waggled rapidly through the nights and early mornings of those two days as I gathered all necessary information and researched the legal requirements and jargon that my document would need to exemplify. I submitted my case brief exactly one year after I discovered that my identity had been stolen and misused. I rushed back to the court to get a government seal stamped onto my document, which would have the date verified in ink. Once I heard the metal click of that stamp, I wanted to let out a huge sigh of relief, kick off my shoes, and celebrate. Little did I know, I had only kicked off another round of fighting with the completion of that document.

Immediately, the court claimed immunity due to their inability to change an error that no one was aware of. I returned to my documents and combed through them meticulously. There I found that in 2007, someone had attempted to strike Patricia Jackson's felonies from my record. This event would have lined up exactly with the efforts of the financial planning broker to subpoena my government records. Someone must have seen the flagrant error under my identification number and attempted to remedy it. Unfortunately, this person failed to document the change and send notification to California's department of justice. In short, the correction only applied to that unique copy of my record, not to all the multiple copies (both digital and physical) that were dispersed across county, city, and state offices. This small drop in what had become a sea of paperwork proved that at least one government employee had known about the identity theft, yet I would continue to pay the consequences for years due to a lack of communication between departments.

Ultimately, the court relies on its claim that I did not meet the filing deadline according to the one-year statute of limitations on my case, this too was a lie. This is the claim they had spent months engineering for themselves with each delay, postponement, extension, and months-away appointment. My fight against these claims continues today, even as I write this book.

While my record is technically expunged, it isn't entirely clean. Anytime a background check is run under my name, the acting party will receive notification in bold print that an expungement has taken place. While this is the lesser of two evils, a notification like this still casts a pall of suspicion over my status as a dependable and trustworthy employee. At the same time, any person who searches my name online has access to the knowledge that I am currently in an active libel lawsuit against the Californian government. I stand strong in my pursuit for justice, but neither of these dark marks on my record has done me any favors when it comes to seeking employment in my chosen career field. For the foreseeable future, my regular life will include phone calls and visits to the California judicial system. I have yet to receive so much as an apology, much less financial or professional reparations. My fight continues.

CHAPTER SUMMARY

- I discover that the state government has placed felonies belonging to a Patricia Jackson under my name.
- I receive a full expungement of my criminal record.
- I am unlawfully abandoned by my chosen attorney less than a week before my statute of limitations expires.
- I file my own official complaint against the state of

California one year to the day after discovering that my identity had been stolen.
- I continue my fight as the D.O.J. files opposing claims against me.

In the next chapter, you will learn how this ongoing legal battle discombobulated my personal life and severely damaged my mental health.

CHAPTER FIVE: THE FALLOUT

IF THIS IS HOW THE U.S. TREATS THE INNOCENT, I CANNOT imagine how it treats people who have actually committed a crime. So many times, I have looked back on my life and tried to find something to blame it on. I play the scenes over and over in my head, hunting for some misgiving or folly that could hold the key to it all. It would almost be easier for me if I had done something to cause this. If I had been scheming or carrying malicious intent, I could look at the many unwarranted tragedies of my life and resign myself to them, viewing them as punishment. But no matter how hard I try, I can't see where I have done anything to deserve the vengeance of a powerful state government. I can't see where I have done anything other than demand fair treatment and justice. It seems as though the justice system would be on my side in this pursuit. Instead, the establishment seeks to silence, minimize, and completely snuff me out.

We've all seen enough *Law & Order* and *Criminal Minds* to know how things work when an American citizen commits a crime. They are tried by a jury of their peers and, if found guilty, put away for a long time. But what happens when the government commits a crime against one of the citizens that pay its salary? What due process is there in a situation like that? I have yet to discover one. So far, the protocol seems to be to delay, deny, and excuse, and even destroy the opponent if necessary.

When I was going through the thick of it following my discovery of Ms. Jackson's felonies under my government ID, I spoke often with my family in Chicago. As much as I relied on my faith and maintained my connections with church and spirituality, I felt like my mind and spirit were breaking with the heavy weight of my disenfranchisement. There were days where I didn't see the point in waking up. Days where my ferocious dedication to justice seemed to waver and die down, and I just didn't have the energy to fight anymore. I felt so helpless. During a conversation with my older sister Sinchie, she noticed how lackluster my voice had become. She encouraged me to see a psychiatrist and consider going on antidepressants. I took her advice.

The doctor prescribed Zoloft and I filled my prescription because I understood that God created prophets and that same God gave us medical doctors. There was nothing on earth that did not belong to the Almighty including science. God can heal with medicine and without medicine, this time I needed help from what medicine would offer me. I had always been wary of mind-altering medications. I led an active lifestyle and had been a vegetarian for nearly two decades, so I felt most healthy when my body was in its natural state. I'm the sort of person who treats a headache with five holistic methods before ever opening the bottle of ibuprofen. I believe in drinking water, getting sun and regular exercise, taking vitamins, and practicing the art of moderation when it comes to alcohol and rich foods. To be faced with a clear orange bottle of Zoloft felt extremely defeating. My life had become intolerable without the help of prescription drugs, and as much as I knew this was a natural response to the sort of stress and life circumstances I was dealing with, I couldn't help but feel like a failure. Nevertheless, I knew I wouldn't find justice from beneath my duvet, so I began to take my daily dose.

For some people, mood stabilizers are the right choice. Those with chemical hormone imbalances and hereditary mental illness may even find their personal collection of Rx bottles empowering. But for me, taking that blue pill every day felt anything but. To see the word ZOLOFT etched into each pill as I lifted it to my mouth served as a reminder that somewhere along the way, I had taken a wrong turn. I questioned each bout of hope and happiness when it swept through my body, wondering whether I was experiencing a true relief from sadness or if the medication was simply doing its job. While Zoloft served its duty by keeping me alert and engaged with life, it was also just another added mental challenge to incorporate something like this into my life. It challenged my relationship with my own body and drove a wedge between myself and my emotions.

Once I had filed my official claim and braced for a barrage of rebuttals from the California Department of Justice, I resumed my dogged hunt for employment. Through no fault of my own, I had become a serial professional monogamist. As the excitement factor in my job prospects decreased, I became increasingly desperate just to find something full-time. As I sifted through job boards, I'd imagine myself in each position and match my extremely overqualified skill sets to the position's description. And of course, once I secured one job or another, I'd over-perform and keep a nearly perfect attendance record. I always arrived early, and only left when the job had been done to a T. I remained exceedingly professional in my dress and my dealings with colleagues and customers, learned procedures quickly, and often surprised my employers with astute suggestions and additions to existing procedures.

How did I find the motivation to overperform, you may ask? It was simple. I knew I'd eventually be terminated in pretty much every position that I accepted. Sure, I tried to keep up hope, but ultimately I entered each occupation with this subconscious knowing that my active lawsuit status and/or my documented criminal record expungement would once again render me jobless. My chronic perfectionism was my way of ensuring that I could accept that inevitable termination without shame or guilt. Despite my intellectual knowledge that these things weren't my fault, my emotions often ran wild with disappointment and hurt when I received a professional rejection. But if I knew I had been overqualified, pristinely dressed, impossibly kind, and impressively intelligent, then I could keep a feeling of security as I moved on from one job to the next, knowing that I had been fired through no fault of my own.

Of course, my first few months in any position were often sprinkled throughout with meaningful praise from my supervisors and well-earned respect from my colleagues. To me, though, none of this positive attention had any credibility, because I knew I could never be a good enough worker to outshine the blemishes on my official documents. I lost my ability to accept compliments because they never held enough weight to keep me gainfully employed. While most of my peers were on their way up a corporate ladder, I was on my way down. I had gone from a high-profile government worker with full travel clearance, to a successful marketing agent, to working for a local nonprofit. At my lowest point, I was the manager of a gas station.

Before I go on, let me clarify something: I do not ascribe worth to human beings based on their net worth or professional prospects. I think that people generally have different priorities and opportunities, and that life lands us all in a particular set of circumstances that has been preemptively carved out for us by God's all-knowing hands. I am certainly not above working in the service industry. I call this my lowest point because of how much and how hard I had worked to gain the qualifications for jobs in my field of expertise. For most of my twenties, it was a rare occasion for me not to be enrolled in one college program or another. I put my blood, sweat, tears, and sleep deprivation into earning degrees in my fields of interest. I wrote hundreds of pages in dissertations, essays, and research papers only to work a minimum wage job. It is only because of my valuable investment in education that I call my stint in the service industry a "low point." Anyone who puts their honest work into achieving a goal would feel slighted when that goal suddenly and inexplicably becomes unattainable. That's how I felt when I heard the jolly ding of that gas station's front door as I stood behind the counter each day. I had spent a decade of my youth collecting qualifications, only to be scanning someone else's Diet Coke and cigarettes at 5:00 AM.

I couldn't help but laugh to myself, thinking about just how far I had fallen from L.A.'s social graces. When I first arrived in this city, I was in a souring entanglement with a famous actor, living in a wealthy neighborhood, and regularly splurging on wine and cheese to visit the local theater performances in Griffith Park. I had made friends often and easily, usually with people who were as equally decorated in achievements, job offers, and financial comfort. I frequented popular restaurants, wore fashionable clothing, and woke up every day to the satisfactory knowledge that I had important work to do. I had a generous budget, a saving plan, and several shiny goals to work toward.

Now, I woke up each morning to put on a uniform and work in the service industry. Some of my more authentic friends still invited me to soirees and trendy dinners, but lots of them had slowly faded into the background once my life became too heavy and afflicted to ignore. Many of these people had worked hard, just like me, so that they could enjoy a carefree life of privilege and luxury. That's where I had been headed, too, once upon a time. But soon, being around me felt anything but carefree for my many social partners. It was no wonder that the ranks of support dwindled.

In a particularly cruel twist of fate, I even lost my job at the gas station. It was a new version of the same old tale. I had been an amazing manager—dependable, punctual, collaborative, hospitable, and clean. But one day, without much of an explanation at all, I was let go. By this point in my life, I didn't want to fight one of Goliath's brothers although I did and won that battle. This victory served as a stepping stone a little up the deep pit. I know, it is very difficult to see the light at the end of the tunnel but God always will have a lamb at the corner. We only need to be focused and trust the way-maker and helper. I didn't want to fight and wonder and be sent to voicemail ten times to know why I'd once again lost a job. It was old news, and I was sick of reading the same copy.

No matter how much I struggled with the effects of governmental negligence, I wasn't exempt from the hard knocks of life. As previously discussed in Chapter Three, I had lost my furry angel, Nna, three years prior to discovering my tainted criminal record. At the same time, my home was in foreclosure, and I struggled to bring in money. I knew that my foster daughter had harmed Nna only to get to me. She had used him as a scapegoat, and now there was nothing standing between her anger and my body. Through God's grace and unconditional forgiveness, I still had as much love for her as ever before. I wanted to see her heal and find light in her life. However, I needed to set a firm boundary in order to maintain my own safety and sanity. Amidst all my personal battles, I desperately needed my home to be a safe haven of serenity for both my spirit and those of the children I fostered.

When I arrived home from the vet's office that day, the girl was on her best behavior. I could tell that she felt some sort of remorse for her actions, or perhaps was shocked by the emotional shockwaves that her anger had sent out through our home. For about a week or so, she completed her chores ritualistically, kept a cheery disposition in each of our interactions, and attended church events with me without complaint. Though she was only a year from 18, she still lacked the maturity to understand how her impulsive actions could have long-lasting consequences. I felt empathy for her but still kept my guard up. I began locking my bedroom door at night and avoided leaving any food or drink unattended around her. It was stressful to be on such a high sensory alert in my own home.

We met with our caseworker following Nna's death to discuss whether I'd continue to house the girl or whether she'd need a new placement. I told the caseworkers that I'd be willing to keep her in my home on the condition that she attend church and Bible study. I believed that the Lord would open her heart and awaken her conscience. I was a minister myself and had found so much healing through God's word. I knew that this child would potentially face more abuse and neglect in someone else's home, and wanted her to stay safe with me where she could continue to grow. The caseworker, however, refused to place this requirement on the child. The girl was free to engage in whatever religious practices she most aligned with, and I didn't have the legal right to force her engagement in any particular ceremony. The girl, who had been so compliant with church attendance since Nna's death, suddenly crossed her arms and changed her tune.

"Yeah!" She nervously looked at the agent through the corner of her eye for reassurance, "See? I don't have to go to church if I don't want to. And I don't want to."

"All right," I said calmly.

I completely understood this stance and accepted it without

conflict, but stood firm on the boundary I had set. If this child wasn't willing to offset her dark religious leanings with the light of God, then I could no longer keep her in my home. She was sent to a new placement a few days after the meeting.

That decision was one of the hardest I had ever made. I knew the system did not treat young women like herself with tenderness, and I prayed for her every night after she left. Yet I felt a sense of peace in my spirit about my choice. I knew that I would be of no use to myself or anyone else if I sacrificed my own sense of safety. My home was a sacred place for me and others. I devoted each corner and wooden beam to healing, positivity, prayer, and God's mighty love. I needed to be able to leave my burdens on the front doorstep when I came home each evening, and I couldn't do that in the presence of a child with deadly anger. I still wish the best for that young girl, who is an adult now, and hope that she has discovered her own path to Love.

My Father's Passing

My dear father, whom I have always revered as a role model and mentor, really struggled to process what was happening to me during my decade of struggles with the government before his death. In even the largest families, children and parents align differently. According to any number of variables, from personality type to hobbies to gender, children always imprint on one parent or the other. To the child, this parent is the center of the universe. Their approval is a salve for even the worst emotional wounds, and their disappointment is to be avoided at all costs. For me, this parent was my father.

After living a life in the upper class of Ibusa, my parents immigrated to the U.S. with high hopes for professional and personal achievement. He instilled these values into me. With each degree earned, dissertation written, and better job acquired, my father's bright smile of pride and joy filled my tank and fueled my future ventures. He and my mother had worked so diligently and had taken such great personal sacrifices in order to support and encourage the dreams of my siblings and me. All they asked in return was that we work hard, hold our heads high, and behave with an aura of class and respect in our daily lives. They wanted us to keep a strong faith in God and show through our intelligence and determination that we were capable of reaching the American dream.

There was no reason for me not to meet these expectations. I came from a prestigious family with intellectual and cultural wealth. I had a vibrant and colorful childhood with diverse educational experiences. As much as I struggled to cope with my sudden loss of social status and respect in the fall of 2004 following the false imprisonment, my father struggled even more. Nearly every heartbreak I had faced in life to that point, he had been able to assuage. When I was sick as a child and young adult, my father could comfort me with warm broth and well wishes. One of my uncles once joked that every weekend they played tennis and my dad had me with him. When someone hurt me or treated me unfairly at school or during childhood games, my father could sympathize with me and turn the event into an important life lesson. When I struggled to balance the workload of a doctorate program, my father could encourage me to see the light at the end of the tunnel by reminding me how far I—and he—had come. I was his little girl, and he had always been able to keep a protective embrace of love surrounding me, no matter how far away I was from Hyde Park, Chicago.

But no matter how he tried, my father just couldn't protect me from the deep-seated poison of racism in America. He couldn't defend me in that park in 2004 from the officer who only saw a person of lesser value when he looked at my face. He couldn't intimidate the California state government into offering better treatment as it repeatedly flicked me away like an unwanted nuisance after destroying my ability to pursue career growth. The power of my father's plentiful love just couldn't penetrate the stone-cold injustices that I faced as an adult lost in the oppression of America's injustice system. And the knowledge of his impotence left my father emotionally crippled.

What I wanted and needed more than anything from my family and friends during those years of confusion, pain, and fighting was simply to be listened to. I needed my loved ones to create space for my sorrow and support me in my efforts to find fairness. My father, an action-oriented man, just couldn't find peace in his spirit, knowing that he was immobile in the face of this vast and spreading issue. So when I saw my father on holidays or spoke with him over the phone, we often avoided the topic of my ongoing struggles with employment and later, my ongoing struggle with correcting the judicial system's error on my criminal record. Instead, we'd discuss his job, upcoming plans, or the state of the American and Nigerian nations. We'd discuss our common interests of politics, current events, and education. It was hard to exclude such a large portion of my daily life from my relationship with my father, but I knew the topic did more harm than good to his psyche. He didn't need the reminder that his little girl was suffering. I never faulted him for that.

In 2012, while I was battling for justice on America's West Coast, my father was teaching mass communications and journalism at a university on Africa's West Coast. He was intelligent and invested in his students and, after decades of service, preparing to retire. While my father was technically of royal blood, he firmly believed that people should be judged on the merit of their character rather than the fame of their associations. He had helped raise his six children to remain humble in their interactions and expect only what they had worked hard to earn.

As his professional life came to a well-deserved close, my father's personal life had become quite tumultuous. According to traditional Igbo practice, my father's oldest brother had been next in line as king. That was until the Ibusan people decided to move away from a monarchic government and toward a more democratic method of selecting leadership. In recent years before my father's death, the custom had changed so that the city's people would come together to choose their next leader out of the royal family. Once he became aware of this shift in traditional customs, my uncle was distraught. He had lived his entire life with the ingrained assumption that he would one day inherit a position of power and wealth without any additional effort on his part. When he realized that he would need to earn that position rather than have it automatically granted, my uncle became a tyrant. His relationships with his siblings and other relatives turned hostile, and he was intoxicated with the idea of reclaiming ultimate power.

I couldn't say exactly what the nature of the conflict was that took my father from this earth, except Cain and Abel. I only know what I witnessed as a child in those years I spent in Nigeria. I know that polygamy can make for a particularly nasty family dynamic. The poisons of jealousy, hatred, and competition can overtake a household in seconds, placing everyone in danger. Not only do the wives engage in personal rivalries, but they also serve as agents for the vengeful desires of their husbands. Once my uncle's thirst for domination trickled down to his wives, my Nigerian family set out on a path of self-destruction. Now the wives of this rightful heir shifted their attention from cooking, cleaning, and child-rearing as means to win his affection to concocting different schemes that would help him secure his position as king. Though my father was only one of many perceived threats to this inheritance, he was enough of a hazard that his sisters-in-law set their sights on harming him in hopes of receiving the reward of their husband's lavish attention.

In a set of circumstances eerily similar to those that had snatched Nna away from me a year earlier, my father was poisoned in mid-December. I received a call that he was coughing and vomiting up blood. Only hours before, I had been speaking on the phone with him about mundane matters of politics and daily life. Now, I received news that brought me to my knees. My mind ran images of Nna's sick body on the floor of my bedroom, shaking and convulsing with the all-consuming pain of poison burning his insides. My heart sank to my stomach, and I sought a safe place to begin supplicating with God for my father's life as he slipped into a coma.

In the Bible, the Lord describes a particular spiritual place that people stay while they're awaiting Judgment Day. In the Catholic tradition, this is called purgatory. There are many depictions of this in-between in classical art and literature. During my hours of intense prayer, I journeyed to this in-between with my father's soul. As I watched him wander and seek peace, I experienced a strong and dark temptation to bargain for my father's earthly survival. I knew that this temptation was not of God's will, so instead of asking for any specific method of physical healing or survival for my dear father, I spoke words of surrender and trust.

"Have Your way in my father's life," I spoke to the Source, "Do with his spirit what You see as just and righteous according to Your will," I repeated desperately. I didn't know where my father's relationship with God stood at the moment of his poisoning. Truthfully, it wasn't my concern. I only knew that I shouldn't bargain my faith for the faith of my father's. As much as I wanted to, I knew I shouldn't pray specifically for his bodily healing. Instead, I held space for his soul as it wafted between the physical and spiritual realms.

For three days, my father remained in a coma in his home village of Nigeria. For three days, I knelt and fasted in prayer. People often remark that, in the midst of near-death experiences, they see their entire lives flash before their eyes. In these 72 hours, images of my relationship with my father through the years flashed before mine. I saw him reading to me as a tiny toddler. I saw him ladling soup into my bowl as we gathered for dinner. I saw him laughing endearingly at the antics of his daughters. I remembered a specific, momentous conversation that had happened between us when I was only nine years old.

In a family with many daughters, there are often roles ascribed to each girl. I had always been the daughter of charm and beauty. I felt comfortable in this role and knew how to play it well. I knew how to twirl my skirts, bat my eyes, and lilt my voice adorably when interested in swaying an adult's decision. After years of this, I was steadily approaching adolescence where these behaviors would take on new and weighty implications. One afternoon out of the clear blue, my father summoned me into the living room. "NK.," he said in his booming tenor, "you must stop relying on your physical beauty to charm me and others. Your beauty will fade, but your brain will always hold your admitting ticket to success. Use it. You are more than one thing, and you can certainly accomplish anything if you give yourself enough credit."

These wise words had shaken me awake from my limited perception of myself and sent me out on a quest for learning and knowledge. My father was the reason I could survive adversity and always find an escape route out of even the most hopeless circumstances, and now his life hung precariously in the balance between vitality and death. On the third day of my father's coma, as I prayed fervently for God's will, I saw on the screen of my closed eyelids a vision of heaven. John 14:2 in the Bible says this: ***In my father's house, there are many mansions. If it were not so, would I have told you that I am going there to prepare a place for you?*** What I saw that day, Christmas Eve of 2012, was a vibrant vision of my deceased relatives gathered in a celestial mansion. Their bodies had been restored to health, and they threw their heads back to laugh together in the joy and freedom of God's paradise. They were in a world void of evil, ill-will, and darkness. Moments later, my phone rang in the next room. My father had died. As much as I grieved for the love of my beloved parent, I knew in the depths of myself that all was well.

CHAPTER SUMMARY

- I fall into a depression after multiple failed attempts to find justice.
- I begin taking prescription antidepressants, which only serve to increase my shame.
- My relationships begin to suffer from the worsening circumstances of my personal life
- I work as a gas station manager and lose that job without explanation,
- I am forced to have my foster daughters moved to a new placement due to one sister's unwillingness to seek deliverance following Nna's violent death.
- My father is poisoned and dies after a three-day coma on Christmas Eve.

In the next chapter, you will learn how I sought healing and rebuilt my life even as I struggled to manage the disastrous effects of my battle with California's state government.

CHAPTER SIX: HEALING

LOSING MY FATHER WAS BOTH AN ADDED HEARTACHE TO MY ongoing Job experience and the impetus for my healing. After experiencing the gravity of my spiritual journey alongside my father's wandering soul, my perception of my own earthly life shifted dramatically. Traveling metaphysically into the spiritual realm had rendered my struggles with the state government trivial in comparison. The entire ordeal had calibrated my mind and emotions to see the mist of my life from the perspective of a loving creator. Rather than focusing as heavily on my next defensive move against a callous and negligent system, I began to focus intentionally on my journey toward healing.

Before tackling larger issues such as occupation and the overarching direction of my life's purpose, I focused on the things in my daily life that needed to change. In the midst of my depression and lack of resources, I had forgotten the joy I often found in spending time outdoors in the sun with Nna. In fact, I hadn't really allowed myself to consider opening up to a new pet at all, despite the fact that Nna's presence in my life had offered me so many opportunities to commune with true purity and innocence of an untainted heart. To face the trauma of what had happened to me in Griffith Park nearly ten years ago, I needed to remind myself how it felt to be untethered in the natural landscape of my home city.

Slowly, cautiously, and full of hope, I resumed my visits to local hiking trails and green parks. Of course, I always checked twice, thrice, four times to be sure I had my identification on my person. But ultimately, I reclaimed my right to the sun, dirt, and jubilant sounds of wildlife. I refused to allow the fear of systemic racism and ill-willed profiling to rob me of something that had always offered me peace and freedom. In addition to this, I began surfing the web for adoptable dogs. I'd visit animal shelter websites and learn the names and faces of these little creatures who were all patiently awaiting their adopters. My heart unfurled and created room to accept another furry friend into my home.

Next on the list was the Zoloft. One morning, as I reached for that infamous white-capped plastic container, I took a good long look at the pills inside. I honored my personal truth; that these pills had been prescribed in an attempt to lessen the pain of a set of external circumstances that neither my psychiatrist nor I could control. Those circumstances didn't seem to be in any rush to change, and I knew that I wasn't a person who struggled on a biochemical level with hormone imbalances in my neurological systems. I knew that the little blue pills in my hand were doing about as much good as a bandage slapped over a gunshot wound. Sure, they slowed the flow of blood a bit, but they did nothing to propel my heart or mind toward true healing. They had robbed me of my ability to trust my own emotions and had stopped the progression of my natural menstrual cycle in the process. My body's natural rhythms had been disrupted for over a year. I needed to make a change.

That day, I called my doctor's office to make an appointment. When the time came, I shared my concerns with her and requested to begin the weaning process off of my prescribed medication. She agreed with me and aided me in slowly tapering off the dosage so that my body had time to equalize. This was, of course, not an easy process for my body. I often experienced mood swings, dry mouth, hair and weight loss and grogginess. Nevertheless, I stuck with my resolution and awaited the day that I could nix that Rx bottle from my daily routine. When it came, I celebrated by having an especially large and delicious breakfast. And later that month, when I felt the old familiar ache of Mother Nature in my womb, I actually sent up a prayer of gratitude and, afterward, chuckled to myself. As a young woman, I never could have predicted that the discomfort of a menstrual cycle would send a sensation of relief through my body. But life's funny like that, I guess.

Once the small details of my life fell into place, I expanded my awareness to the larger, more substantial decisions that I needed to make. What new career path would I forge for myself that could thrive in the face of a stained government record? How would I ensure that my primary emotion in life was joy, gratitude, and peace? This would take a considerable amount of pondering and prayer. Once again, I settled in at the celestial conference table to meet with God on this particular topic. I felt nudged to consider going into ministerial service full-time. "But," I interjected in the solace of my mind, "there are so many ways to serve the church, God. Which way should I choose?"

In the still, small, humble way that the Lord speaks, I heard my answer. I had been so in tune with God's will during my father's last days. My prophetic gift kept me supernaturally in touch with the cosmic affairs of life after death. I would be a hospital chaplain, counseling patients and family members through end-of-life care and preparation. I would pray over and spiritually guide both births and deaths for all denominations. But first, I needed to attend seminary and earn my Master's Degree in Divinity. This was a basic requirement for just about every revered hospital in the area.

Once I accepted God's call on my life in my mind and spirit, I needed to take the next steps to accept it in the physical realm. With most of my resources exhausted from years of university and a particularly nasty court battle, I sighed in exasperation. As is my natural way, I closed my eyes and bowed my head and I was thrown into an open vision. And, I am in a classroom. "A classroom? No, I am done with schooling. For crying out loud, I have a PH.D. But God was the Almighty, so, before the day was over, my resolve was, "Okay God," I said hesitantly, "If You want me to go back to school, I need You to pay for it." This felt like a bold ask and an improbable one, but I knew that I couldn't fund this venture myself and didn't want to take out any loans. Once I spoke my desires to the Lord, I got to work applying to different Clinical Pastoral Education (CPE) and seminaries. Faith without works is dead!

As strong as my faith is in the Savior, I knew that God wouldn't rain down a blessing of thousands onto my front stoop without my additional effort. This is a principle I have carried throughout my life, from girlhood to adulthood. I have no doubt in my mind that prayer is powerful, and that God hears every desire of my heart if I am bold enough to speak them aloud. I rest assured in Matthew 7:8 *For every one that asketh receiveth; and he that seeketh findeth; and to him that knocketh it shall be opened.* The Lord wants nothing more than to see the children of God thrive and live life to the fullest. However, I never ask for something I'm not willing to work for in my own life. I asked God to pay for my Master's Degree, and once I rose off my knees and opened my eyes, I began writing application essays and devoting at least an hour a day to pursuing admission.

I applied first to Cedars-Sinai CPE Program in L.A. but received no confirmation that my paperwork had received an interview. I moved my attention to Children's Hospital Los Angeles, where I soon received a call to come in for an in-person interview. I dressed sharply and arrived promptly, having mixed emotions about the old familiar feeling of the interview process. So many times, I had swiped mascara over my eyes, spread color over my lips, and buttoned myself into a blazer only to sweat through a souring job interview and receive a rejection devoid of explanation. So many times, I had interviewed, received a job or an appointment, and later been let go for vague reasons. The whole process of sliding into business casual clothing, fixing my hair, and clicking my heels down a tiled hallway had begun to carry implications of anxiety and rejection. On the day of that first CHLA interview, I was elated to learn that I had been granted a second.

During my second interview there with the hospital board, my excitement carried me away into conversations about my personal faith and how it would render me suitable as the chaplain for this medical facility. Alas, my vocabulary had gotten too advanced and my fervor perhaps too intense, because I received feedback following the meeting that my speech and vocabulary may be too "advanced" for a hospital where most patients were young children, immigrants and teens. I both understood this take and regretted it because I had been truly excited at the idea of joining my passion for protecting and supporting children in need while leaning on my deep and personal relationship with God to help patients reach their own relationships with the Holy Spirit.

After this experience, I kept my head up and moved forward. I began speaking with the many colleagues and acquaintances from my past professional endeavors. I leaned on my network and ended up rekindling a connection with a coworker/friend Afe Maison from the U.S. Department of Commerce. Her husband PK Thompson was training at Union Seminary at the time, and he shared with me that his uncle ran the chaplaincy program at Providence Little Company of Mary Hospital and that he'd be glad to put in a good word for me. This little hospital south of the city was in need of good ministers. They called me to schedule an interview, and by the end of that week, I had not only been accepted into the chaplaincy program but had been awarded a full-ride scholarship for all the Clinical Pastoral Education classes I'd need to take as a resident chaplain, plus the necessary coursework to gain my Master's in Divinity. God had answered my prayers after all, I just had to accept and put one foot after another believing that my prayers were already answered because it had been answered ahead of me; 'faith without works is indeed dead. The problem with us many times is that we ask for something but then we allow doubt to steal it away yet and still wanting. Just believe and leave it upon God to answer, 'yes', 'no' or 'not right now,' refuse to allow the fox that steals; doubt takes it away.

Going into this new career, I felt like my purpose was to give. I had been naturally placing myself in healing roles since I was a young woman. I had set out to heal foster children, to heal Nna, and regrettably, even to heal a few romantic partners. This was a gift that I had been developing and honing in on for decades. So naturally, when I felt God's call on my life to work as a religious guide in a hospital setting, everything made sense. But God's plan extended far past using me as a servant. God doesn't just want healing for others through me—the Spirit wants to heal me through unconditional love. As a resident chaplain, I had room and board and a new well-meaning community.

Half of CPE training is what you'd expect—learning about bedside manner, how to respectfully interact with bereft family members, and how to approach spiritual conversations in an inclusive way. This is the giving half. The other half of the training is about receiving. It's spending time with professional mental health counselors who approach inner wounds from a biblical standpoint. It's about cultivating a safe space inside oneself as a spiritual guide and healing old wounds that could potentially impede the work of chaplaincy. I had essentially gained surprise access to free therapy with highly qualified professionals, along with three colleagues turned brothers, Father IKechukwu, Chaplain Rone-iff Carr, Father Chris, Abraham, Chaplain Dreya, and our mentor-professor and friend Teleso and all the wonderful chaplains caregivers and Leadership team at Providence all made the experience amazing. And the Chaplain Mary-Beth who kept buying me clothes throughout my residency was definitely God sent. Through the hand of God, I received the priceless gift of spiritual healing—something I had never expected.

After weaning off of Zoloft for the first time, I experienced another dip in mental health and personal function. My goal had always been to live each day without the assistance of mind-altering pharmaceuticals, but I also knew better than to play tough to my own detriment. So I got back on a low dose. During these intensive therapy sessions, however, I was able to wean once again. As I've said before, I used Zoloft when I got into the sea of depression and felt the water rush over my head. I didn't know how to heal myself from the inside out. I didn't know how to ask myself the right questions or allow my scariest memories and emotions to run their course. But with the help of a compassionate professional, the ragged scars on my soul began to smooth over and heal from within. For that reason, I look back on my chaplaincy training as a time of light, joy, and the sacred work of reunifying my mind, heart, and body.

Once I completed my CPE classes, I enrolled in seminary coursework to receive my MDiv. That's what I spend most of my time doing now. I still cannot find suitable employment to manage my daily grocery and travel costs. I continue to build my resume and seek employers who will see through my tainted records to the resilient person underneath. At the same time, I am deepening my knowledge of the Bible and God's ways more right now than ever before in my life. I soak up each lesson like an eager sponge, genuinely enthusiastic about learning more about the only One who matters in this short human life. I am surrounded by people who want to see me succeed. The people in my daily life consistently take time out of their days to pour into me, to mentor me, and to facilitate my continued growth. I cannot deny that there is unfinished business on the outside of my life, but I no longer walk around feeling there's unfinished business in my inner world. I know my worth as a child of God. I know I am unconditionally loved and forgiven and take great pleasure in sharing this message with others.

I preach monthly at my new church home, City of Refuge, and attend services weekly. The only salve for a suffering heart I've found is to ease the suffering of another. That's why I take the time each month to cook and serve homemade dinners to 200 homeless individuals. I wish I had the means to feed them daily, but I choose to be content in the knowledge that I am at least filling hungry bellies once a month. No matter what I've gone through, I've never been able to stop my mind from dreaming and goal-setting, so of course, I have a couple of hopes in mind for this community service endeavor. Eventually, I hope to have food trucks planted throughout the city that will serve meals to L.A.'s homeless population on a much broader and more frequent scale.

I have gained regulars and love seeing the relief on their faces when they come to collect their NK Specials. My heart for homeless people is that they would learn and understand the vocabulary surrounding their mental struggles. I seek to help them feel less alone as they face inevitable bouts of depression, anxiety, addiction, and maybe even suicidal thoughts. I think that many people who struggle in this area can find it difficult to create a separation between their real selves and the selves they become under the influence of a cognitive disorder or neurological imbalance. Sadly, many of the people I interact with on a daily basis haven't even come to the realization, an awareness of his or her neurological deficit or psychiatric condition for themselves (this condition is known as Anosognisia). Mental illness doesn't define any of us as human beings and is just another example of human weakness that can be made holy through the love of community and the love of an omnipotent God.

Following my father's death, my youngest sister was left without care. My father had remarried following his divorce from my stepmother and had a little girl called ChukwuNwazimo, my half-sister. She was born in a Nigerian hospital where, during her delivery into the world, she was not given enough oxygen in the birth canal. This single event, which occurred before my little sister had even seen the light of day, left her with some cognitive delays and physical disabilities. At the time of my father's death, ChukwuNwazimo was only four years old. My father, who had been caring for her impeccably for all of her life, suddenly became incapacitated following his untimely death in 2012. This is what motivated me to shift my focus from parenting foster children in a temporary home placement to starting a full-out home for children with disabilities. I wanted to be able to care for my sister with the best resources available by obtaining the necessary licensing to start a nonprofit organization.

Unfortunately, I could not obtain these requirements in order to take over my sister's daily needs. I suspect that the marks on my criminal record and the indication of an expungement paired with my active status as a plaintiff in a libel lawsuit against the state disqualified me from establishing a nonprofit and working with disabled youth. I still struggle today with the overwhelming conviction that I could have and should have done more to ensure that my sister had all the opportunities that she deserves. ChukwuNwazimo is 11 years old now and lives with her mother. She is a continual reminder to me that new beginnings and hope can never die, as long as new generations continue rising to God's call on their lives.

In 2017, after five years of stagnancy at the city level with my case, I decided to file my case with the California Supreme Court. Of course, I faced many of the same manipulations and delaying tactics that I had already faced in smaller arenas. In fact, this juncture of my journey to justice may have solidified for me more than any other experience that the government was not acting professionally or even logically in its dealings with me and my case.

The attorney I was working with to file at the Supreme Court level one day requested that I gather fresh copies of my documents for him to work with. This seemed logical, as my files had been through the hands of many attorneys and judges by that point. Once again, I headed up to the government offices to sit in frigid air conditioning and await my turn at the clerk's desk.

Once I arrived and shared my identification information, the clerks began to whisper amongst themselves quite unprofessionally. Clearly, something had appeared on their computer screens that rendered my presence in the office quite interesting. I felt as though I had time-traveled back to junior high as the two female clerks lifted their hands to cover their mouths and spoke in hushed tones. I didn't know what to do, so I continued to stand at the desk and await further information or instruction regarding my requests for documents.

"One moment," said one of the clerks with a disingenuous smile.

She went behind a partition and left me waiting. Soon she brought out with her a large man who appeared to be some sort of manager in that department of the court's dealings. He held a folder in his hands that looked to be sealed with the government's stamp.

"Do you mind joining me outside?" he asked cautiously.

Confused, I offered him a simple "sure."

There in the cold and isolated hallway, the man passed over my documents. I dropped my pretense of patience and immediately opened the paper envelope to take a look. What I held in my hands was more proof of illegal evidence tampering. There should have been no difference between these documents and those that I had at my home besides the presence or absence of pen and pencil markings from the many people who had looked over them to work on my case. I was extremely well-acquainted with my court documents, as I had spent hours upon hours thumbing through them, reading and rereading their clauses, and leaving notes in their margins.

So, of course, I immediately noticed the multitude of discrepancies as I flipped through my fresh copies. I saw that changes had been made to documents of mine that had been created as far back as 2005. Each item in my file had a government seal that showed the year and date of each addition or subtraction—or at least they should have. Yet I saw gaping holes where information favoring my freedom had been removed and saw added text that favored the government's point of view. And none of these changes had been accurately reported by a new and updated government seal.

I had been taken out of the populated clerk's office so that no one there would see my reaction to blatant forgery on behalf of California state government employees. The cold hard truth of my situation had been lost in a he said-she said battle of black and white ink and massive loads of paperwork. I couldn't believe my eyes. I left promptly, and my lawyer left me just as quickly once he had seen the insidious amendments to my documents. Anyone could recognize the obvious changes if they only held the worn copies of my documents next to their freshly printed counterparts. While they were supposedly identical copies, they both reported entirely different series of events.

My attorney's part with the fraud was done and he didn't want to have any part of this, as he could easily lose his license to practice if he were framed for tampering with official court documents. I reported him to the California Bar Association, again they requested that I provide the original documents. Not surprising, that at the end of their supposed investigations they sided with H. Foxy, and that the $100 he offered to me for making sure my documents disappeared was good enough. I began to feel much like the lady in Charlotte Perkins Gilman's short story "The Yellow Wallpaper." In it, a woman's husband decides that she has lost her mind, and the more she tries to convince him that she hasn't, the crazier he believes her to be. Ultimately her lack of control over her own life and her husband's refusal to listen to her drives the wife to actual insanity, at which point the husband sits smugly in what he believes is a triumph of accuracy.

The state government was doing the same to me. It had decided that I wasn't an upstanding citizen worthy of fair treatment, and the more I begged and pleaded and tried to prove my innocence, the more innocent guilty it believed me to be. As I walked out the double glass doors of that building with severely botched documents swinging in my left hand, I worried for myself. I wondered how long I could keep my footing in the sane world while a massive force of wealth and social power seemed determined to undermine my credibility and cut down my right to citizen's justice. I reconfigured myself and my case and ultimately filed successfully with the Supreme Court of California.

My case currently sits in the hands of the highest state officials in California's judicial system, and I will not give up as I continue to pray each day that God will move their hearts to serve justice. My case now is likened to the The Parable of the Unjust Judge as told by Lord Jesus The Christ in the book of Luke (18-1-8). In it, a judge who lacks compassion is repeatedly approached by a poor persistent widow seeking justice. I am the elect therefore God will bring justice. Any microscopic loss of pride that the L.A. courts may endure certainly will not outweigh the overwhelming evidence in my life that this particular string of careless mistakes has caused grave damage to my personal, spiritual, mental, and financial wellbeing.

Now and always, I will seek the light. Even in the most hopeless situations, healing is available. For the rest of my life, I'll be on a quest to find it.

CHAPTER SUMMARY

- I revisit my old hobbies of hiking and spending time in nature
- I wean off Zoloft for the first time and find equilibrium in my body
- I receive a full-ride scholarship to become a resident

chaplain at Providence Little Company of Mary Hospital after receiving a word from God to pursue this field
- I receive intensive therapy through my Clinical Pastoral Education
- I file my case with the California Supreme Court

In the next chapter, you will learn about the many loose ends that remain untied in my life due to this decades-long battle against racial profiling and clerical negligence in the L.A. judicial system.

CHAPTER SEVEN: LOOSE ENDS

RIGHT NOW, AS I CONCLUDE THE TELLING OF A STORY THAT I can only wish had been fiction, I am visiting my family in Chicago. When the global pandemic of COVID-19 set in, I was in the midst of completing my Master's Degree in Divinity. As stay-at-home orders spread across the nation, all my coursework was transferred to a digital medium as my peers and I were encouraged by our university to quarantine indefinitely. This meant I would be sitting in my apartment alone for days, weeks, and perhaps even months on end with only my television, computer, and cell phone to connect me to the outside world. In the early days of the virus outbreak, most of the U.S. didn't fully understand what precautions we needed to take to stay safe. As for myself, I tried to minimize my contact with public spaces as much as possible. I even had my daily necessities delivered to my home to minimize person-to-person contact. The only semblance of normalcy that remained in my life, and certainly the lives of many others across the globe, was the expectation that I would complete my coursework through the seminary as I continued to pursue my MDiv online.

Soon, the isolation began to deplete my emotional resources. For many people who live alone without a partner, child, or pet, it can feel depressing. And became lethargic, unenthusiastic, inexplicably exhausted, and unmotivated but this is opposed to my state of mind as I check into my classes online. I am not at all lonely, understimulated, and lacking direction even though I had in the past wrestled with dark emotions as I thought about how this veritable halt in the normal hustle and bustle of L.A. life might have affected the homeless people whom I was used to cooking for, the foster children who were in less than ideal home placements, and even the senior citizens who were at high risk of infection and could no longer engage with the outside world whatsoever. I couldn't stop thinking about what fearful consequences might result from families being forced to stay in one home together when an abusive partner or parent was in the mix. I couldn't stop wondering whether the usual nonprofit organizations that my homeless friends relied on were still in operation, or if these people were now battling starvation and food shortages among their usual difficulties.

The days began to bleed together as I woke up morning after morning in the same empty apartment, milled about from bed to couch to kitchen all day, and turned back into my bed each night. Before lockdown, I was already on my schedule of reading the whole Bible by December. So, I was mental and spiritually prepared and fed. So while many were giving their 2020, you are going to get this and get that, God had revealed opposition and I warmed my family, friends and social media friends to prepare for the opposite but to seek, pray, and repent. There was going to be a lot of crying. Like I've seen in so many movie montages, I could practically see the pages on my calendar being flipped away one after the other in rapid succession. All the little interactions that we as humans rely on in order to feel a sense of belonging and union had been snatched away from us in an instant. There were no more smiles and niceties exchanged over the grocery counter, no more subtle smiles passed back and forth between strangers on the street.

I couldn't collaborate in person with my fellow students in the seminary program during my time in the college classrooms, couldn't find any comfort in the clamor of shoes and backpacks and side conversations as we all rose to leave that classroom at the same time. I spent more hours scrolling through social media than I had ever even thought possible, as this was the only place that I could remind myself about others' existence in the world alongside me. Mostly what I learned from these social media escapades was that every person, no matter their background, had the distinct feeling that they were the only person on an island of seclusion. Ironically, especially in L.A., many were stacked in apartments and very physically near while simultaneously feeling worlds away from civilization.

Nothing productive could come from me continuing this quarantine alone, and according to the news media, there was no end in sight. I chose to flip my perception of the situation so that I saw it as an opportunity rather than a hardship. An opportunity for what, you may ask? To see my many relatives in Chicago and enjoy the communion of mundane daily tasks together. I decided to drive first to the North Side before heading to Hyde Park and stay with my older sister and her family for a while. That is where I have been then to Hyde Park then the suburbs to see my mother and step dad for several weeks, and where I will stay for quite a few more. Instead of waking up to an eerily silent one-bedroom apartment, I wake up in my parent's home to the sound of their feet sticking to the kitchen tiles as my mother prepares the first pot of coffee. Instead of wasting away in the gray drudgery of my own thoughts and aloneness, I enjoy the wagging, yapping, and tongue lolling of my younger sister and cousin Abosde's two small dogs. I eat dinner at a dining table rather than from a container on my own couch, and often have laughs and shared experiences over delicious home-cooked Nigerian cuisine.

Since my older sister Dr. Sinchie and her husband Emmauel are essential workers, they still must leave home each day to go to work. I, as a full-time student, am able to stay home and complete my required readings and assignments. This allows me to spend lots of time with the two dogs, which have reminded me just how wonderful it can be to live life alongside a wholesome furry friend. When I need to take breaks or just want to feel the sun, I leash the pair of pooches up and take them out for walks around the neighborhood. The three of us have developed a fast friendship, and I often tease my sister and cousin that their dogs might begin to favor my company over theirs.

For the first time in a long time, I feel like I can take deep breaths.

When I found myself standing before a judge in 2004 to accept grave penalties for an insignificant transgression, I grieved more than anything the loss of my identity as an achiever. For all my life, I have taken great pride in my diligence and my ability to collaborate with just about anyone to get a job done. Nothing keeps me going quite like the sense of purpose that I felt when I was climbing corporate ladders, creating sturdy professional networks, and traveling often to handle important business matters. While some may look upon the corporate environment or the world of entrepreneurship as a rat race, I look on them as a safe haven for those of us who enjoy an executive dress code, a strong cup of coffee or chai tea, and strategic interactions over conference room tables.

I thrive in these competitive environments and always have. So when I helplessly watched my credibility as a business professional drain away from me due to a botched criminal record, it felt a lot like being left behind in a foot race. I watched as my peers, mentors, and even mentees passed me by and grew smaller as they moved closer to the horizon. Meanwhile, I constantly had the sensation of running frantically through sludge. I wanted to be neck and neck with the best in business and finance, but instead, I was miles behind the fray in the muck and mud of something I could not change or undo.

But when a worldwide quarantine swept the nation, and even the most straight-laced executives were forced to slow life down to a domestic pace, my need to keep up with the Joneses subsided. The constant pressure I have felt for the past two decades to prove my worth, attain better employment, and reclaim my position as a highly coveted and skilled professional seemed to have been relieved through some invisible valve. For once, we were all in it together. Stay-at-home moms and CEOs alike were forced to stay behind their own front doors in loungewear for months on end. There was no such thing as better or worse, more productive or less. The pandemic threw a curveball to everyone, and no one blamed anyone for not knowing how to handle it. While I continued to fear for those in dangerous situations, I also took a huge sigh of relief as my competitors slowed down to match my pace. For once, I didn't feel like I was being outrun.

My step-father Edward and mother, who served faithfully for 35 years as a government social worker, are just overjoyed to have all her children in the same vicinity once again. The downfall to raising hard working children geared toward accomplishing great things is that, most often, those great things take them in all sorts of different directions. Our large family hadn't been in one zip code at the same time since 1992 before coronavirus called us all home. It has been so refreshing to take a first-row seat to the lives of my mother, my stepdad, and my siblings. The woes and mercies of my own life feel much less consuming when I can also witness the lives of my loved ones as they play out day after day. When I visit my mother's home, I most often hear about the goings-on of her husband's family business, which he started a few years back with a couple of his close friends as partners.

I listen as my stepfather discusses the state of his business and how he will strategically ensure that the pandemic, which has been fairly catastrophic to many industries and to the economy as a whole, does not bring his business down with it as well. I have enjoyed putting my mind into problem-solving mode as the two of us toss ideas back and forth about how to maximize resources and continue finding clients who need his service. My stepfather has actually mentioned a few times that he'd like to have me come on as a director in his company at some point. Due to my independent nature, I had never considered reaching out to family members to find a suitable job, I had never quite detailed what has happened to me in Los Angeles to my mother until this visit, so all these seem to have fallen right in my lap. Who knows? Maybe once I've gone through the requirements to become a Chaplain, I'll consider moving to the Midwest to offer my input and personal labor to this family business. It would allow me to stay plugged into my family on a deeper level, and my mind would receive all the stimulation and competition that I have been missing since I began struggling to find employment.

Being in my old hometown has helped me come back to my roots. My mother's larger kitchen space allows me to enjoy cooking the way I used to. I experiment with all my old favorites in her home, remembering the flavors and spices of my childhood spent in Chicago and Nigeria. A slower-paced life allows for more meditative cooking, and I enjoy the colors and sensations of each vegetable as I chop for egusi soup or the strategically round puff, puff, the sizzle of oil in a pan, and the way a bundle of herbs can light up a room with nostalgic smells if a person only adds a little heat. Each morning I start my day by praying and reading my Bible, as these avenues for connection with God have sustained me through even the worst of times.

Interestingly enough, the role of America's police force has been a prevalent topic of discussion in our nation today. There are many differing opinions, the most extreme of which involve defunding law enforcement departments (a Democratic mission) and, on the other end, increasing budgets for police forces so that they can enjoy higher pay and more protective gear. As for me, I don't necessarily come down on either side. If I truly believe in God's power and almighty plan for my life, I cannot walk around in fear of anything—not even a police officer. The Lord gave me a spirit of trust and perhaps even naivete, so I don't define any person by the uniform they wear or the roles they inhabit on a professional level. I guess I give people the benefit of the doubt and assume they have goodwill until they prove otherwise. I can say, however, that when I see a person in law enforcement in my daily life, whether that be on the roads, in public spaces, or walking past me on the street, I **never** expect extraordinary kindness.

The culture of America's law enforcement is not one of selflessness and community service, but rather one of strategic resource guarding and defensiveness. I see that those who desire to enter the world of law enforcement most often do it out of a need or hunger for authority. This is a job that magnetically attracts people who want to hold power over others when it should be a job that attracts gifted servants and protectors. I cannot hold hate in my heart for any person, but I can point out the clear issues in a government entity's philosophy. I think that our police force trains its officers to follow a problematic philosophy and that, until we revisit and amend the tenets of that ideology, our so-called protectors will often prey on the vulnerabilities and weaknesses of impoverished minorities while they worship and comply with the motives of the rich majority.

Truth be told, I love the country in which I emerged. Else, I wouldn't stay here. But I believe that a true patriot tells the truth about the flaws of its nation so that these flaws can be addressed and remedied. I'm a strong proponent of the idea that you cannot heal what you do not acknowledge. As of right now, we live in a nation that claims to be the land of the free, a country governed by and for the people. Our country stakes its reputation on the idea that anyone who enters it can bring an American Dream to fruition. The USA is supposed to be teeming with opportunities that any person can take advantage of in order to build a family legacy. Instead, our country strategically mutes and disenfranchises a vast portion of its loyal citizens. This freedom and equality is actually conditional based on race, ethnicity, religion, class, and orientation. It seems to me that those who hold power in this country are willing to keep it at all costs, even if that means committing violence, erasure, or even betraying the tenets of its own constitution.

Thus far in the U.S., we have been enabling our leaders to continue in the delusion that our nation is a paradise of possibilities. Today, I am encouraged by what I'm seeing. Today, I see that many protestors and activists are refusing to enable any longer. Today, the people are holding their governors accountable to uphold the ideals on which our country was founded centuries ago. I know that I am not afforded the same leniency as my white peers. I know that I cannot expect any favors, forgivenesses, or allowances from law enforcement, while a white person in the same situation may not even be stopped at all. But I refuse to live in fear. I cannot sacrifice my peace of heart and mind for anything; else I'll be rendered completely ineffective.

As for my own case, it remains open as far as I am concerned. Yes, I have had my record expunged. But I have not been recognized whatsoever as a victim of any wrongdoing. I have been erased, ignored, and dishonored. What happened to me may seem small in the eyes of those who have seen footage of police officers murdering Black people in cold blood, or have seen the bruises of an innocent man beaten with nightsticks. I'd like to propose that it all matters. I think the violence committed against minorities by law enforcement officers is so blatantly wrong that fighters for the cause of equality lean on those instances as verifiable proof that America's justice system is twisted. These are the cases that cannot be ignored, argued, or denied. They are tragedies that simply should not have happened. Our opponents—those who choose to close their eyes to the gross and twisted social inequalities that fill their pockets—are so adamant that nothing is wrong that these horrific images and videos seem to be the only effective tools for jolting them awake. However, there are thousands of people just like me who are victims of a racist system that disenfranchises minorities in a million subtle ways before it ever kills them. I want justice for us too.

If there's anything I could say to help others understand the gravity of bureaucratic oppression, it's this: I'm you. I grew up in love. I had and have a long life full of intricate memories, childhood games, romance gained and lost, passions ignited and snuffed out. I work hard, I have goals and dreams. I have something to offer. I attended both private and a state university, and I spent my twenties dazzled by the lights of big cities. We are one and the same. And then one day, out of the blue and with no provocation, I lost it all. I lost my ability to be carefree. I had the American Dream snatched from my hands, without warning, over an unclipped leash. I have suffered the repercussions for decades. If this could happen to me, it could happen to anyone.

Who knows how many manila folders sit, covered in gray dust, in the filing cabinets of state courthouses all across this country? And who knows how many of them hold proof of injustice and disenfranchisement inside their paper folds? They all symbolize living, breathing human beings who have lost their professional credibility due to racial profiling or bureaucratic blacklisting. Each of these manila folders is a person who walks through his or her daily life shouldering the judgment of privileged people who don't understand how insidious a system can be when it's not on your side. We're condemned for needing government assistance, for not having better occupations, for not being able to climb out of the mire that systemic racism has cast us into and, all the while, we're innocent.

All I want for myself, for other victims like me, and for this country as a whole is for light to be shed on the truth. I want to reconcile what has happened to me with the Californian government in a way that feels final and authentic. I want to be able to resume my life as an achiever of great things without a blemished reputation. I want to be able to walk into the DMV, into a nonprofit organization as a volunteer, or into a job interview without worrying about whether the supervisors will believe me when I tell them that I am not a dangerous criminal. I don't want special treatment or undue honors—I just don't want to continue paying the consequences for a sin that isn't mine to repent. I feel that I have been wrongfully convicted and that I'll never be released from my cell. Except, rather than living my days in a prison of concrete and metal, I have lived them in a prison of questioning looks, hurtful assumptions, careless rejections, and the overwhelming sorrow of being left alone while others rush unimpeded toward the light.

There was a time in my life where I would watch the news, television, and crime documentaries where a person's innocence hung in the balance. I'd often think to myself, "This person must have done something wrong at some point; otherwise they wouldn't be in this sticky situation." And, in a black and white world, that might be true. If right was always right and wrong was always wrong, if no heroes turned to villains and no villains worked undercover for the good guys, that sort of mentality might be accurate. But the world we live in deposits almost everything in the gray area. I did nothing wrong, yet found myself in a precarious situation. There are prisoners on death row who are innocent of the crime with which they've been charged. There are venerated religious, political, and executive leaders who lead lives of evil and darkness behind the scenes. If I've learned anything from my experience with the government, it's to always look deeper than my first judgment of a person. In a broken justice system, what is meant to be ordered turns to chaos. Because of racism, classism, and money-motivated politics, a criminal charge doesn't mean guilt any more than a priestly vestment means innocence.

My hope is that together, our nation can become a congregation of truth seekers. I hope that everyone from neighbors to hiring managers to the president considers that no person can be fully defined by the way they look "on paper." I hope that we all offer one another an olive branch of allyship and, in the meantime, that we take a good long look at the poisonous dealings of our very broken justice system. I hope that we gather strength in numbers and stand in lines, however unbearable, at the polling booths for each election. I hope that we reignite each of our God-given desires for genuine human connection and act in love before denying in fear. I hope that we drive out darkness with the light of firm, valiant honesty and that we bring all people, righteous, sinful, and all those in between, to justice. I hope I'm next on the list for that. I hope I'll see the day in my lifetime where my record isn't called into question before I'm allowed to pursue a dream.

And reader, I hope you'll help me get there.

CHAPTER SUMMARY

- The coronavirus pandemic sends me into quarantine, where I decide to take a trip back home to Chicago to stay for a few months
- I discuss my plans for the future and the possibility of moving home to work at my stepfather's family business.
- I share my thoughts on the state of America's law enforcement and how my experience affects my relationship with the police force on a daily basis.
- I disclose the state of my libel case and my hopes for reconciliation.

FINAL WORDS

TODAY AND FOR THE PAST FOUR YEARS, OUR NATION HAS RISEN into political upheaval over the election of a reality television host to the executive office of the presidency. Donald Trump, a person with documented racist, sexist, and even criminal behavior has completely overturned the expectation for dignity and professionalism that we have demanded from our presidents since 1776. He speaks impulsively and crassly, rarely answers a direct question, and views the inner workings of our democratic nation as a business venture. While we were all surprised, including himself, when I learned of his election in 2016, I do see that some good has come from his term in the White House, the truth finally bubbled up into the light.

Before Trump, our nation hid its racism, classism, and self-serving motivations under the guise of diplomacy, education, and false patriotism. The only people who were consistently aware of the unfairness of our nation's law and law enforcement were those who directly suffered the consequences, i.e., racial, ethnic, and religious minorities, as well as those in the lower class of wealth. Our leaders masqueraded their harmful ideologies as good intentions. Every speech was shrouded in stately poise, and every proclamation made in intellectual sophistication. Then came New York's rough and tumble real estate mogul into the Oval Office.

President Donald Trump is either too dense or too glib to cast over his narcissism and greed with a veil of politeness and diplomacy. And though we've suffered greatly due to his carelessness, the masses are finally becoming aware and educated on the topics that most minorities and impoverished people have been screaming about for decades. Those with socioeconomic privilege are beginning to see past their preferred security and into the dark underbelly of intolerance that our nation has begun to personify. This summer began with one of the longest nationwide protests in history. And this time, it wasn't only the oppressed who took the time to march. Those who have in the past chosen to ignore the pain of their brothers and sisters in order to preserve their perceived comfort instead chose, this June, to listen, witness the generational pain of our nation, and do something about it. Donald Trump's inability to manipulate the masses has pulled the curtain back on a long history of malicious leadership. Because of his presidency, the people have come to understand that their democracy is now and has for a long time been under imminent threat from America's elites. Truthfully, the bigoted motivations of Trump's voters may have actually done the rest of us a favor by electing a leader who isn't able to play the same manipulative games as his predecessors.

Now that what was in the darkness has come to light, and that lady liberty is not blind, she actually can see. Yet, it's our responsibility as a people to begin the restoration process. I remember Maslow's hierarchy of needs, which shows us that as humans, we must first meet our physical needs before we can begin to grow our emotional and mental stamina. In keeping with this principle, our first course of action as a nation has to be securing the rights of all people to live without a threat of violence or death in the country that they occupy. This means that we need to remove the excess privileges of law enforcement officers to beat and kill men and women of color and that we need to persecute them according to natural law for their sadistic crimes. The constitution states that no man is above the law, yet many have gone unpunished for even the basest of offenses.

Once we have ensured that all are safe in this nation, we must make it our mission to see the people reflected in leadership. Congress, the Senate, the President, and the Supreme Court must be an accurate representation of the people they serve. No political office should be for life. It simply is not wise. The world needs younger leadership with strong elders as mentors, That means at least half will be female, and that we increase the representation of Hispanic, Asian, and African-American citizens in federal, state, and city leadership offices. Up to this point, the white male voice has dominated all decision-making endeavors for the American nation, and, in an effort to keep their power, this white male administration has actively boxed out the voices of those that don't match their demographic. Once we change that, we'll begin to see a much more rounded series of conversations occurring on the highest levels of government.

The United States of America has talked the talk since the day we won the Revolutionary War. We've rattled on and on about how free we are, how collaborative, how inundated with opportunity and uplifted by an inclusive mentality. Yet we have never walked the walk. My hope for this nation is that we will join together in this new decade to take our first real steps together.

I wrote this book to make sure that this narrative—my narrative—is not excluded from the revolution that I hope to see play out before me in the near future. At a time when the privileged among us are lending their ears to an ongoing fight for equality, I wanted to take my time to speak my truth. Oppression absolutely looks like red blood on the streets, it absolutely sounds like a shower of gunshots being directed at persons with black and brown skin, and it absolutely smells like tear gas. But, in my experience, oppression can also look like the inside of a small county jail. It can sound like a vague and awkward rejection from an employer over the phone. It can smell like the fresh ink on a newly printed criminal record, which has been botched and fabricated by faceless agents inside a circumspect system. Oppression can certainly look like a war between David and Goliath, but it can also look like a stack of paperwork and a maze of red tape.

As our nation rises up to claim its rightful inheritance of unequivocal freedom and well-enforced equity among citizens, I hope that it won't forget the thousands of us who are caught in a web of "clerical errors." There are the faces on the news that capture our attention and sympathy, but there is also a great magnitude of faces that never make it onto primetime television. We are the faces behind the systems that too often prevail over the innocent underdog. As you and I march into a New Age, I hope that I, and people like me, can see their records cleared, their dreams restored, and their lives revitalized.

For all the dreamers who can't dream, the students who cannot learn, and the laborers who cannot find work, I will do my part. By demanding justice for myself, I demand it for you too. I won't stop…

www.ingramcontent.com/pod-product-compliance
Lightning Source LLC
Chambersburg PA
CBHW072206100526
44589CB00015B/2398